LEATHER
& BEAD

JEWELLERY TO MAKE

LEATHER
& BEAD
JEWELLERY TO MAKE

Cat Horn

Search Press

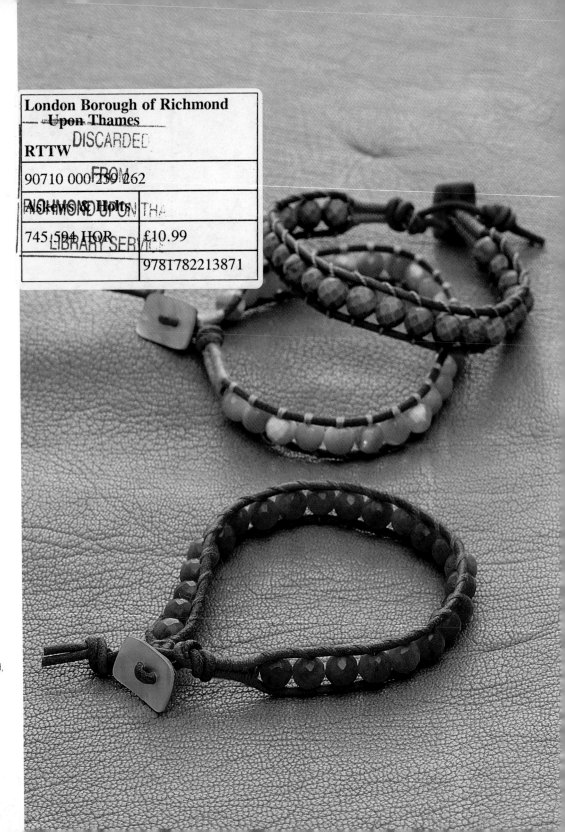

A QUARTO BOOK

Published in 2016 by
Search Press Ltd
Wellwood
North Farm Road
Tunbridge Wells
Kent TN2 3DR

ISBN: 978-1-78221-387-1

Conceived, designed and produced by:
Quarto Publishing plc
The Old Brewery
6 Blundell Street
London N7 9BH

QUAR.LABJ

Editor: Michelle Pickering
Art director: Caroline Guest
Designer: Elizabeth Healey
Step photographer: Guy Ambrosino
Project photographer: Emma Robinson
Indexer: Diana LeCore
Creative director: Moira Clinch
Publisher: Paul Carslake

Colour separation by PICA Digital Pte Ltd,
Singapore
Printed by 1010 Printing International
Ltd, China

CONTENTS

INTRODUCTION

Hi!

I am Cat Horn, the designer behind Cat Horn Accessory on Etsy, a handcrafted jewellery and accessories shop that offers playful, everyday accessories that are fashionable and fun to wear. I love unique jewellery and have a passion for handmade products that show the voice of the person who crafted them.

I have been making jewellery since I was a little kid. A long family vacation to the American Southwest when I was ten years old introduced me to the world of beadweaving on a loom, and from there I fell in love. The intricate designs made with colourful beads woven into jewellery and clothing excited me and drove me to learn how to make them myself. Leather and glass beads were my first – and are still some of my favourite – jewellery supplies as a result of this trip, and they inspired many of the projects in this book.

Years later, I trained as a fashion designer and worked in the New York fashion industry, right in the heart of Manhattan. When I was not working on the next year's line, I was spending my lunch breaks and weekends in bead shops filled with endless rows of juicy beads and sparkling jewellery supplies, stocking up for my dream job. After five years, I left New York and the big fashion industry behind to start my own business in the incredibly creative and artistic city of Philadelphia, Pennsylvania. Here, I learned the ropes of production-style jewellery making by working part time for local jewellery designers, while building my own Etsy store and discovering my own style.

I love making things with my hands. There is something incredibly satisfying about looking at a finished creation and saying 'I did that'. That feeling is kind of a sugar rush. In this book, I want to share with you the skills my teachers have taught me, including some unique tricks for working with leathers, cords and beads. The projects begin with simple pieces that use basic skills like stringing, then build on those skills to create some pretty impressive beginner pieces. More challenging techniques like weaving and macramé are then added to the mix, and finally all of these skills are combined to create showstopping designs. By the end, my hope is that I will have helped you build the confidence to take on more complex pieces, and inspired you to design jewellery that expresses your own personal sense of style. So, let's start creating together!

I like to organise my beads and findings into clear containers and label them to make it easier to find what I want. Wooden pegs are useful for storing reels of cords and threads.

ABOUT THIS BOOK

This book features 33 projects for making beautiful leather and bead jewellery, including necklaces, bracelets and earrings.

Chapter 1 describes the tools and materials used to make the projects and explains key techniques step by step. If you are a beginner and want to practise a technique before embarking on a project, then this is the place to go. If you already have some experience, then use this chapter as a reference tool whenever you need to. At the end of the chapter you will find advice and helpful hints on designing your own jewellery.

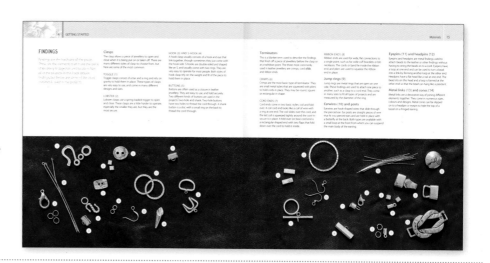

Chapter 2 is where you'll find all the projects. These are divided into four sections. The first section includes basic projects that use simple stringing and knotting techniques, and is the ideal place for a beginner to start. The second section features jewellery constructed using braiding and weaving techniques. In the third section, you can develop your knotting skills with a selection of macramé projects. The chapter finishes with a flourish, with a final section of mixed-technique projects that will challenge your jewellery-making skills.

Skill level

You don't need any prior knowledge of jewellery making to try any of the projects in this book, but some require more concentration than others.

Skill level graded from 1 to 3

Photograph of the finished piece of jewellery

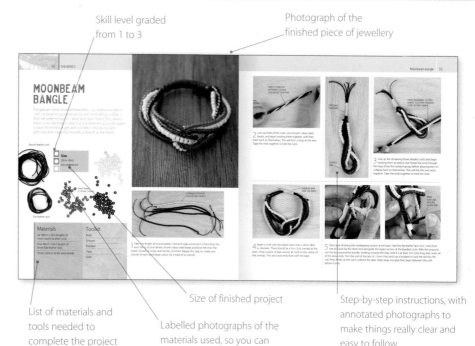

List of materials and tools needed to complete the project

Size of finished project

Labelled photographs of the materials used, so you can identify exactly what's needed

Step-by-step instructions, with annotated photographs to make things really clear and easy to follow

Level 1: Quick and easy; ideal for a beginner

Level 2: More concentration and time required

Level 3: More challenging techniques

CHAPTER 1

GETTING STARTED

Having the right materials and tools is an essential part of creating a beautiful piece of jewellery. This chapter provides an overview of the main tools and materials used to make the projects in this book. The core skills you will need are also explained, from simple stringing techniques and knots to the fundamentals of braiding, weaving and macramé. Even if you have never made your own jewellery before, these techniques will get you started on the road to making beautiful leather and bead jewellery.

MATERIALS

TOOLS

TECHNIQUES

DESIGN

MATERIALS

Learning about the different types of leather and the wide variety of beads and findings available will help you choose the best materials for the project you wish to make. More advice on choosing materials to suit a particular design is given on page 30.

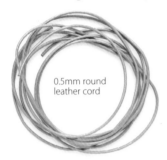

0.5mm round leather cord

LEATHER AND CORDS

The main materials used to make the jewellery in this book are leather laces and cords, which can be strung with beads, knotted, braided or woven together in a multitude of ways. Silk and nylon are used when a finer cord or thread is required.

Leather and suede

Leather refers to the skin of an animal that has been tanned and preserved, and often coloured with dyes. Usually it has a smooth side, often with a pebbly texture, and a rougher, textured side that is referred to as suede. Suede is really just a specific texture of leather. The suede finish is actually the rough inner surface that is left once the smooth outer layer of the leather has been stripped away. Three types of leather and suede are used to make the jewellery in this book: cords, laces and scraps.

3mm flat deer-hide leather lace

ROUND LEATHER CORD

Round leather cords come in a variety of colours, including metallic ones. Some cords are softer and more supple than others, depending on the thickness of the cord and how it has been prepared. Because of this quality, it is good for braiding, macramé and stringing. Round cords are measured by diameter, often in millimetres – for example, 0.5mm, 1mm, 1.5mm.

FLAT LACE

Suede, leather and rawhide laces fall into the category of flat lace, and they are measured by their width. The thickness varies, with suede and leather laces being 1–2mm thick, while rawhide tends to be much thicker. Suede and leather laces tend to be softer and easier to manipulate. Rawhide lace is tougher and will behave more like round leather cord in most projects. The softness of the leather depends on the type of hide used. For example, deer-hide leather lace is much softer than regular leather lace, which is usually cowhide. Depending on the design, flat laces can be used for braiding, the softer laces for macramé and the tougher laces as the warp cord in weaving.

LEATHER AND SUEDE SCRAPS

Leather and suede scraps are the trimmings of the leather or suede hide that are too small to be used for larger items like bags or clothing. They are much cheaper than buying a large section of hide. For

1mm round leather cord

Synthetic alternatives

Vegan leather, pleather and ultra-suede are synthetic materials that have the look and feel of real leather, but are entirely man-made. Very good faux leather can often be indistinguishable from the real thing. Synthetic versions of all the cords, laces and leathers used in this book are readily available.

jewellery projects, they are the perfect size for finishing techniques such as binding raw ends, or they can be cut to shape to create focal pieces.

Silk cord and thread

Silk is a natural fibre spun by silk worms to create their cocoons. Despite its delicate appearance, it is very strong, with a higher tensile strength than steel. This means that it takes a lot of weight to snap the cord. Silk also takes dyes very well, and the resulting colours are vibrant and last a very long time. Silk cords and threads are sold either on spools or in 1.8m (2yd) sections wound around a card with a needle attached. Depending on the manufacturer, the thickness is indicated with either a number or a letter. The higher the number or letter, the thicker the cord. For example, #4 silk is thicker than #2, and F silk is thicker than C.

Nylon cord and thread

Nylon is a synthetic material that is very strong and comes in a variety of colours. Because it is synthetic, it resists fading and rot over time. Another interesting feature is that high heat from a thread burner can be used to melt or seal the ends for a finish without glue. Just like silk, nylon comes either on spools or in 1.8m (2yd) sections with a needle attached. The thickness may be indicated in millimetres or by a number or letter system, as with silk.

0.5mm round leather cord

3mm flat deer-hide leather lace

3mm flat suede lace

1mm round leather cord

3mm flat rawhide lace

1.5mm round leather cord

1mm round leather cord

3mm flat leather lace

Silk and nylon cord and thread

#3 nylon thread

#14 silk cord

#6 silk thread

#14 nylon cord

#3 silk thread

BEADS

The options for beads are endless. They are made from a variety of materials and come in every shape and colour imaginable.

Types of beads

The term *seed bead* refers to any small bead. The most common type is round (these are generally referred to simply as seed beads), but other shapes are also widely available. A numbering system is used to indicate the size of seed beads; the smaller the number, the larger the bead – #6 seed beads are larger than #11, for example. Other beads are usually measured in millimetres. For round beads, they are measured by their diameter. For other shapes, two measurements are given, usually the width and length of the bead. Beads can be made from many different materials. The beads used in this book can be classified into three basic categories: natural, metal, and glass and plastic.

NATURAL BEADS (A–D)
Natural beads include semiprecious and precious gemstones (A), pearls, wood (B), bone (C), horn and shell. All of these materials are found in nature. The bead is either polished or cut from one of these materials into the desired shape and drilled with a hole for stringing. Because these beads are natural, they are not always consistent in size or colour, and the hole sizes can vary greatly, depending on the quality. Sometimes they are also enhanced in some artificial way to either strengthen or bring out the qualities of the material. Beads made from materials such as wood may also be coloured, including metallic finishes (D).

METAL BEADS (E)
Metal beads are made from many different metals and can range in price from very expensive to affordable, depending on what type of metal they are made from. At the higher end are beads made from solid precious metals, such as sterling silver, gold and rose gold. The middle range beads tend to be made from plated metals, which are base metals like copper, brass and steel with a precious-

metal coating. At the more affordable end of the scale are the solid base metals. All of these are great options, depending on your personal taste and budget.

GLASS AND PLASTIC BEADS (F–G)
Glass (F) and plastic beads can be very simple in appearance or artfully designed with intricate patterns, and they can be made to mimic many natural beads, such as pearls (G). They come in a huge variety of shapes, sizes and colours, including metallic, and they can have a much greater consistency of overall size and hole size than beads made from natural materials.

In the selection of beads shown below, the letters refer to the material each bead is made from (see left), and the numbers to the shape or style of the bead (see right).

Bead shapes and styles

Beads are available in such a huge range of shapes and designs that the choices can seem overwhelming at first. The following types have been used in the projects in this book:

 Round (1) – the most commonly used bead shape, ranging from tiny seed beads to crystal-encrusted statement beads

 Oval (2) – oval-shaped beads

 Tube (3) – tubular-shaped beads (larger than bugles)

 Bugle (4) – long, narrow, tubular seed beads available in several hole sizes and in a range of lengths

 Drop (5) – teardrop-shaped beads designed to dangle

 Spike (6) – beads shaped like a spike, with the hole drilled horizontally across the wider end (referred to as top-drilled), or drilled vertically from top to bottom

 Faceted (7) – beads cut with multiple flat faces in a geometric pattern for a sparkling effect

 Chips (8) – small chips of semiprecious stones in irregular shapes

 Charms (9) – decorative beads that come in a multitude of sizes and shapes, from stars and hearts to feathers and flowers

 Rondelle (10) – flattened round beads, with a wide range of hole sizes

 Crow (11) – basically large, round seed beads, usually made of glass, plastic or wood

 Heishi (12) – small disc-shaped or tubular beads made from natural materials, such as shell, stone or wood

 Focal stone/bead – a statement stone or bead designed to be the focal point of a piece of jewellery

FINDINGS

Findings are the hardware of the piece. These are the elements that make the piece of jewellery fit together and function. Not all of the projects in this book require findings, but below are some of the most commonly used in the projects.

Clasps

The clasp allows a piece of jewellery to open and close when it is being put on or taken off. There are many different styles of clasp to choose from, but here are some of the most common.

TOGGLE (1)
Toggle clasps consist of a bar and a ring and rely on gravity to hold them in place. These types of clasps are very easy to use, and come in many different designs and sizes.

LOBSTER (2)
Lobster clasps use a spring-loaded trigger to open and close. These clasps are a little harder to operate, especially the smaller they are, but they are the most secure.

HOOK (3) AND S-HOOK (4)
A hook clasp usually consists of a hook and eye that link together, though sometimes they just come with the hook side. S-hooks are double-sided and shaped like an S, and usually come with two rings. They are very easy to operate for most people. Both styles of hook clasp rely on the weight and fit of the piece to hold them in place.

BUTTONS (5)
Buttons are often used as a closure in leather jewellery. They are easy to use, and hold securely. Two different kinds of buttons are used in the projects: two-hole and shank. Two-hole buttons have two holes to thread the cord through. A shank button is a disc with a small ring on the back to thread the cord through.

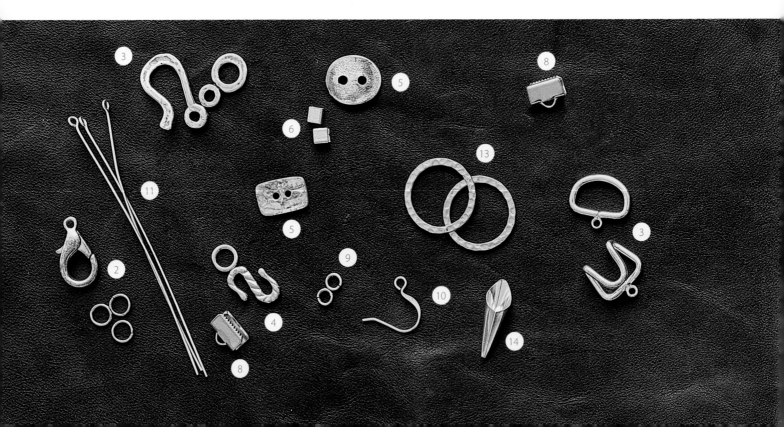

Terminators

This is a blanket term used to describe the findings that finish off a piece of jewellery before the clasp or at a transition point. The three most commonly used in leather jewellery are crimps, cord ends and ribbon ends.

CRIMPS (6)

Crimps are the most basic type of terminator. They are small metal tubes that are squeezed with pliers to hold cords in place. They may be round, square or rectangular in shape.

CORD ENDS (7)

Cord ends come in two basic styles: coil and fold-over. A coil cord end looks like a coil of wire with a ring at one end. The coil slides over the cord, and the last coil is squeezed tightly around the cord to secure it in place. A fold-over (or box) cord end is a rectangular-shaped end with two flaps that fold down over the cord to hold it inside.

RIBBON ENDS (8)

Ribbon ends are used for wide, flat connections to a single point, such as for wide cuff bracelets or bib necklaces. The cords or band lie inside the ribbon end, and pliers are used to squeeze the ribbon end in place.

Jump rings (9)

Jump rings are metal rings that are open on one side. These findings are used to attach one piece to another, such as a clasp to a cord end. They come in many sizes to fit all types of projects and are measured by the diameter of the ring.

Earwires (10) and posts

Earwires are hook-shaped wires that slide through the pierced ear. Ear posts are straight pieces of wire that fit into pierced ears and are held in place with a butterfly at the back. Both types are available with a small loop at the front from which you can suspend the main body of the earring.

Eyepins (11) and headpins (12)

Eyepins and headpins are metal findings used to attach beads to the leather or other findings without having to string the beads on to a cord. Eyepins have a loop at one end and can be used to turn a bead into a link by forming another loop at the other end. Headpins have a flat head like a nail at one end. The bead sits on this head and a loop is formed at the other end so that the bead can hang like a pendant.

Metal links (13) and cones (14)

Metal links are a decorative way of joining different elements together. They come in numerous sizes, colours and designs. Metal cones can be slipped on to a headpin or eyepin to hide the top of a tassel on a fringed earring.

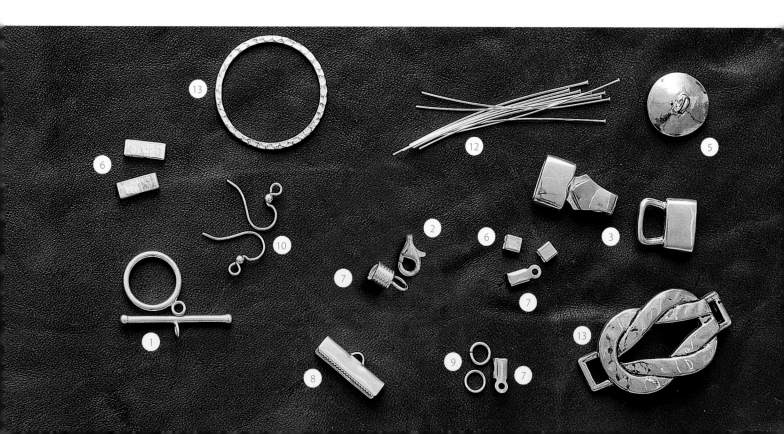

TOOLKIT

Having the right tools for the job is just as important as having the right materials. Luckily, leather jewellery does not require expensive or hard-to-find tools – you probably already have most of them around your home. The following list includes the tools used most often in the construction of the projects in this book.

Pliers

Jewellery pliers come in all shapes and sizes, but what is important is finding a pair that feel comfortable to use and that fit the type of jewellery you are making. The following three basic pliers are all you need in order to get started.

CHAIN-NOSE PLIERS (1)

Chain-nose pliers are the type you will use most often to make jewellery. These pliers are smooth and flat on the inside, and come to a point at the end. Chain-nose pliers are used to hold things that are too small to grasp with your fingers, such as when opening and closing a jump ring. They are also used to crimp cord ends in place.

CUTTING PLIERS OR WIRE CUTTERS (2)

These are very helpful in trimming the extra wire from headpins and eyepins. It is important to note that wire cutters should only be used to cut wire. Never use them to cut paper, cords or leather, because this will dull the cutting edge very quickly. There are a couple of different kinds of wire cutters. The cutting edge can be on the side, like a pair of scissors, or on the top. Either type can be used in most instances, but depending on the situation, one may be easier to use than the other. Side cutters have been used in the projects in this book because they

are best for getting into small spaces and trimming away extra wire. However, feel free to use whichever kind of cutter works best for you.

ROUND-NOSE PLIERS (3)

Round-nose pliers are only used in a few of the upcoming projects, since they are used for a very specific job, but they are a handy tool to have in your jewellery-making toolkit. As the name suggests, these pliers have round noses that come to a point at the end. These cone-shaped noses are used to create round loops in wire, such as on headpins and eyepins. Round-nose pliers can have one or two round noses. Pliers with one round nose have the advantage that they do not leave marks on the wire, but the drawback is that only one side of the pliers can be used to form a loop. Double-sided round-nose pliers are reversible, meaning both sides of the pliers can be used to wrap. Either type is perfectly fine to use for the projects.

Tweezers (4)

Tweezers with a long pointy nose are very handy for basic knotting projects, allowing you to direct the knots to exactly where you want them.

Bradawl (5)

A bradawl is a long, pointed metal tool that is helpful for teasing knots out of cords, as well as for poking holes in scraps of leather. When a knot does not land exactly where you want it, you can insert the tip of the bradawl into the knot and gently pry it open. To create a hole in leather, gently poke the bradawl through the leather until it comes out the other side. Bradawls are usually very sharp, so be careful.

Scissors (6)

Since leather is a pretty tough material, you will need good, sharp scissors that give a clean-cut edge. Also, just like with a good pair of wire cutters, do not use them for cutting other things, such as paper, because this will dull them very quickly.

Beading needles (7)

Beading needles are thin needles, much thinner than sewing needles, and they often have large eyes. They come in different sizes, ranging from fine to heavy, and it is always helpful to have an assortment of different sizes on hand. Twisted beading needles with collapsible eyes are easy to thread, and they hold the cord tightly as you bead.

Ruler (8)

Keep a ruler on hand for measuring throughout all of the following projects. Any kind will do, but a longer ruler is handier than a short one.

Thread burner

A thread burner is a battery-operated tool with a filament that heats up and is used to melt the ends of nylon cord. A thread burner is very handy but, if you don't have one, glue will work just fine.

Glue (9)

Depending on the situation, different types of glue are better than others. Regardless of the project, though, it is best to use glue with a precise application tip for better control, because in most cases the places needing the glue will be very small. Drying time is also an important factor to consider. For some projects, you will want the glue to dry slowly, giving you time to complete the steps or clean up overflow. Other times, it is best for the project to set immediately, so a quick-drying glue would be better.

Masking or painter's tape (10)

Tape is used throughout the projects to hold elements down as you work, and to bind braided ends together until they can be finished with a cord end. Any kind of desk tape will do the job, but masking or painter's tape is ideal, since the adhesive is not as strong and is meant to be removed. This means that it will not leave a residue on your finished project or worktop.

Bead reamer and thread conditioner

A bead reamer is a narrow, round file. It is useful for smoothing out the holes in beads if they are a little rough for stringing, and can slightly enlarge the holes as well. Thread conditioner or beeswax is applied to silk and nylon threads as a protective coating, with the added benefit of keeping the threads tangle-free.

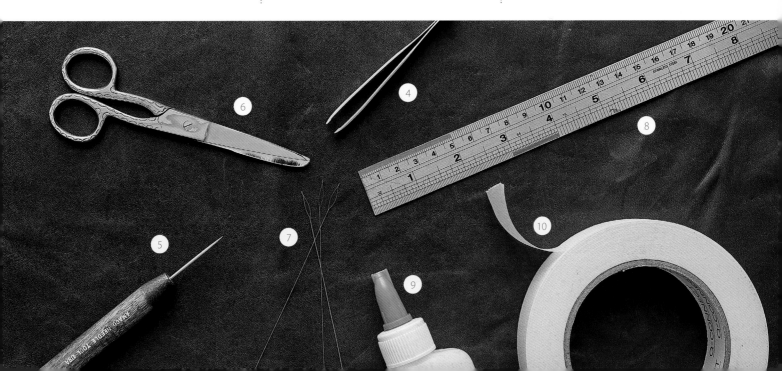

BASIC TECHNIQUES

Basic jewellery-making techniques are the foundation of making leather jewellery. Even if you have never made your own jewellery before, you will quickly be able to learn the core skills needed.

STRINGING

Stringing is the simple act of adding beads to a cord or thread, either by stringing them directly on to the cord or using a needle. However, before the beads can be strung, a little preparation work must be done.

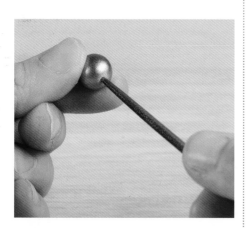

Reaming

Sometimes the holes in beads are a little too small or rough to string, in which case you can use a bead reamer to make the hole a little larger and smooth out the edges. A bead reamer is basically a round file that comes to a very sharp point. Fancier models come with interchangeable tips for different hole sizes. Simply insert and twist the reamer in the hole on both sides of the bead. Not all beads require reaming, and it is important to note that reaming will only make the hole slightly larger, so if the bead still does not fit after being reamed, you may need a thinner cord.

Stretching

No matter what, always stretch out the cords and threads before you use them. This applies to all types of leather, silk and nylon. This will prevent stretching over time due to the weight of the beads, and it takes out any kinks or twists in the cords. Also, stretching allows you to test the strength of the cord. If it snaps easily or gives too much, do not use that section, because it will probably be too weak. To stretch, gently tug on the cord with your hands, pulling in opposite directions. Work on small sections of the cord at a time, moving along the entire length.

Conditioning

Silk and nylon cords and threads should be conditioned before use. Conditioning coats the cord or thread with a waxy or slippery substance that allows tangles to be pulled loose easily. It also helps to protect the thread through the life of the finished project. Either a thread conditioner or beeswax can be used. To coat the cord, simply pull the full length through the conditioner or wax, and then run the cord between your fingers a few times to evenly coat and remove any excess.

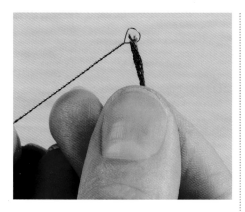

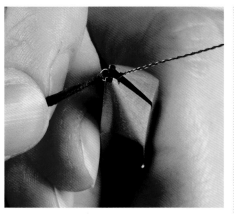

Using a beading needle

1 The twisted beading needles used in this book have large eyes that are easy to thread. Trim off any frayed ends and thread the end of the cord through the needle's eye.

2 Use chain-nose pliers to squeeze the eye closed, or simply slide a bead over the eye to close it over the cord. String as many beads on to the cord as required, taking care to thread them in the correct order.

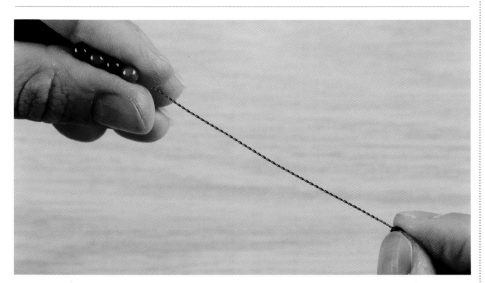

Stringing multiple beads

Sometimes beads come already strung on a piece of plastic cord or thread. This is useful when you want to string beads more than one at a time. First, cut or untie one end of the bead strand and grasp about three or four beads between your thumb and forefinger. Making sure that you keep the beads in line, pull them off the strand in one unit. The holes should still be lined up. Now, thread the needle and cord through all of the beads at once.

Using 'self' needles

For braided cords, it is sometimes helpful to bind the ends of the cords together with tape to create a 'self' needle. First, tightly wrap the ends with a small piece of masking tape, then cut the cords at an angle to make a point. This technique also works well on leather cords to give them a sturdier end to push through tight beads.

SIMPLE KNOTS

You are probably already familiar with these simple knots, but you might not know that they actually have names. The following four knots are used throughout the projects.

Tip: You can use tweezers to position an overhand knot exactly where you want it to go. Begin forming the knot in the usual way, but before pulling the knot tight, slide the tip of the tweezers through the loop and grab the place on the cord where you want the knot to land. Hold the tweezers in place as you pull the knot tight, only removing them when the knot is in position.

PULL TAIL END THROUGH WRAP

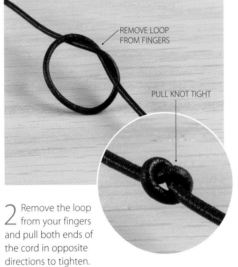

REMOVE LOOP FROM FINGERS

PULL KNOT TIGHT

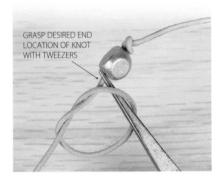

GRASP DESIRED END LOCATION OF KNOT WITH TWEEZERS

Overhand knot

1 This is just a regular, everyday knot. Wrap the cord around your index and middle fingers once, then slide the tail end through the loop you just created.

2 Remove the loop from your fingers and pull both ends of the cord in opposite directions to tighten.

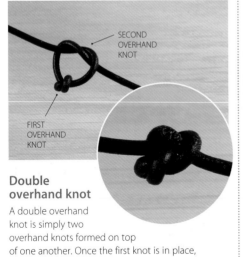

SECOND OVERHAND KNOT

FIRST OVERHAND KNOT

Double overhand knot

A double overhand knot is simply two overhand knots formed on top of one another. Once the first knot is in place, tie the two ends together again and pull the second knot tight.

PULL TAIL END THROUGH LOOPS

Barrel knot

1 A barrel knot looks kind of like a barrel when it is completed, and it is often used as a slider knot (a sliding adjustable knot that acts as a clasp). To form a barrel knot, wrap the cord around your index and middle fingers three or more times, then pull the tail end through the centre of the loops.

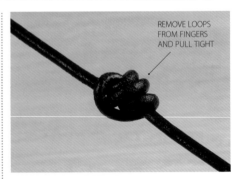

REMOVE LOOPS FROM FINGERS AND PULL TIGHT

2 To tighten, remove the loops from your fingers and gently pull on both ends of the cord, wiggling the knot as it collapses so that the wrapped loops all tighten together.

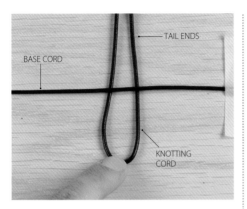

TAIL ENDS

BASE CORD

KNOTTING CORD

Lark's head knot

1 A lark's head knot is often used to attach one cord to another or to a finding. Start by folding the knotting cord in half to form a loop, then pass the loop under the other cord (the base cord).

TAKE TAIL ENDS OVER BASE CORD AND THROUGH LOOP

2 Take both tail ends of the knotting cord over the base cord and through the loop, then tighten.

PULL KNOT TIGHT

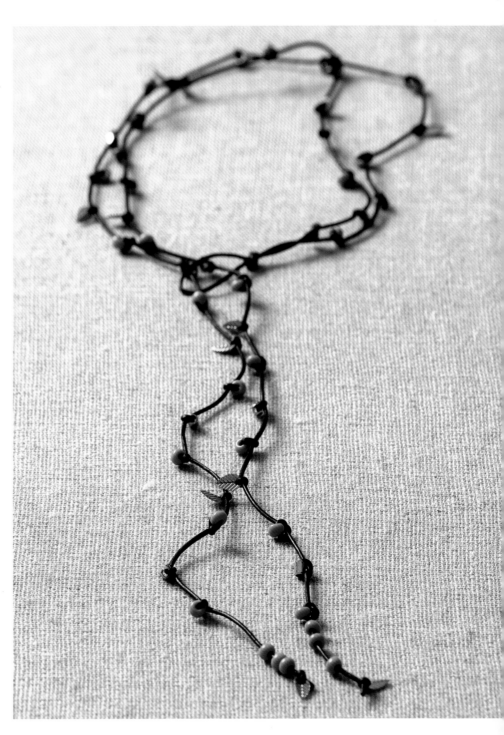

MACRAMÉ

Macramé is the art of knotting, and there are many different types of knots used. The projects in this book focus on some of the most common macramé knots, plus a few more decorative ones. The three that are used most often in the projects are the half-hitch knot, lark's head sennit knot and square knot.

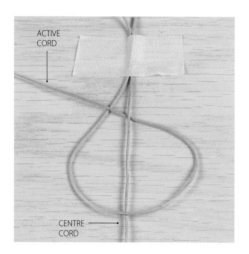

ACTIVE CORD

CENTRE CORD

Half-hitch knot

1 The half-hitch knot is a loose knot that coils one cord around another, creating a helix shape. For this knot there is an active cord and a centre cord. Tape down both cords at the top of the workspace, and just the centre cord at the bottom. Pull the centre cord taut and begin with the active cord on the left. Lay the active cord over the centre cord, leaving an opening between them on the left side. Thread the active cord under the centre cord from the right and up through the opening on the left.

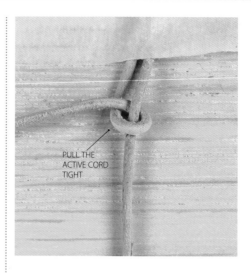

PULL THE ACTIVE CORD TIGHT

2 Pull the active cord tight to complete the knot.

Lark's head sennit knot

1 A lark's head sennit is another way to form a lark's head knot (see page 21). It is often used to create a row of lark's head knots side by side for a bound buttonhole. For this knot there is an active cord and a centre cord. Tape down both cords at the top of the workspace, and just the centre cord at the bottom. This knot is done in two halves. The first half is exactly the same as a half-hitch knot, so start by following the steps shown above.

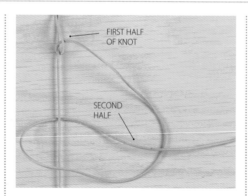

FIRST HALF OF KNOT

SECOND HALF

2 The second half of the knot is a reverse of the first. This time start with the active cord on the right side and lay it over the centre cord, leaving an opening between them on the right. Thread the active cord under the centre cord and up through the opening on the right side.

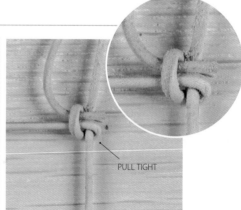

PULL TIGHT

3 Pull the knot tight, and you will see that you have formed a lark's head knot over the centre cord. To form a row, continue alternating left and right until the desired length is reached.

Square knot

A square knot is a two-part knot that forms a little square shape when pulled tight. There are two ways to form this knot. One is with a cord at the centre, and one is without.

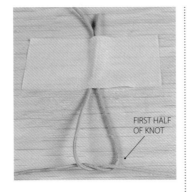

FIRST HALF OF KNOT

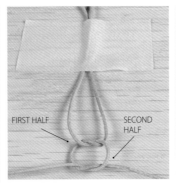

FIRST HALF   SECOND HALF

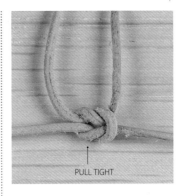

PULL TIGHT

WITHOUT A CENTRE CORD

1 Tape the ends of two cords to the worktop. Lay the left cord over the right, then pass it under the right cord and up through the opening between them. Pull both cords evenly in opposite directions to tighten. (It is not tightened in the next photograph so you can see both halves clearly.)

2 The second half is a reverse of the first half. Lay the right cord over the left, then pass it under the left cord and up through the opening between them.

3 Pull both cords equally in opposite directions to tighten the knot.

WITH A CENTRE CORD

1 You will need three cords to make a square knot with a cord at the centre. Tape down all three at the top of the workspace, but only tape the centre cord at the bottom. Take the left cord and lay it over the centre cord. Take the right cord and lay it over the tail of the left cord, then pass it under the centre cord and up through the opening between the left and centre cords. Pull both cords equally in opposite directions. (It is not tightened in the first two photographs here so that you can see both halves of the knot clearly.)

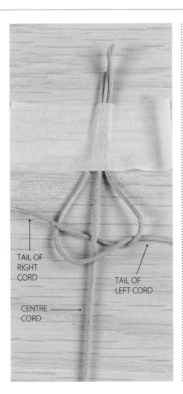

TAIL OF RIGHT CORD

TAIL OF LEFT CORD

CENTRE CORD

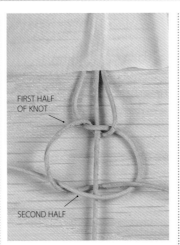

FIRST HALF OF KNOT

SECOND HALF

PULL TIGHT

2 Reverse the first half to complete the knot by laying the right cord over the centre cord. Take the left cord and lay it over the tail end of the right cord, then pass it under the centre cord and up through the opening between the right and centre cords.

3 Pull both cords equally in opposite directions to tighten the knot.

BRAIDING AND WEAVING

Two simple types of braid used in several projects are a standard three-strand braid and a fishtail braid. Loom-style weaving, which involves weaving a weft thread back and forth through warp threads with beads in between, is also used in several projects.

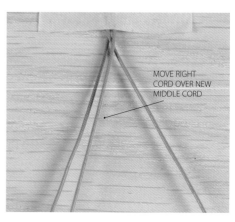

MOVE RIGHT CORD OVER NEW MIDDLE CORD

3 Next take the right cord, laying it over the new middle cord and placing it between the middle and left cords.

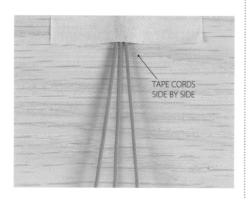

TAPE CORDS SIDE BY SIDE

Three-strand braid

1 A three-strand braid is the most basic type of braid, forming a chevron-shaped weave. Each strand of the braid can be composed of one or more cords. Begin by taping the ends of three cords (or three groups of cords) to the workspace and separate out all three cords.

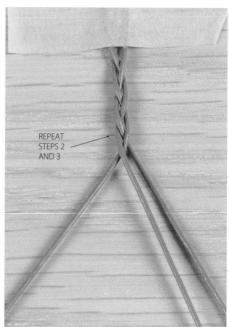

REPEAT STEPS 2 AND 3

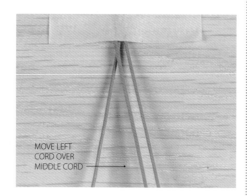

MOVE LEFT CORD OVER MIDDLE CORD

2 Take the left cord and lay it over the middle cord, placing it between the middle and right cords.

4 Repeat steps 2–3 until the braid reaches the desired length.

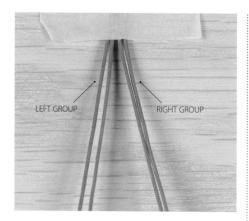

Fishtail braid

1 A fishtail braid can be done with four or more strands. It creates the same chevron pattern as a three-strand braid, but is often much thicker. Begin by taping the ends of the cords to the worktop. Divide the cords into two sections, the left and right groups, and lay the cords out flat within each group.

2 Take the far left cord from the left group and lay it across the other cord (or cords) of the left group and to the inside of the right group.

3 Take the far right cord from the right group and pass it over the other cords of the right group and to the inside of the left group. Repeat steps 2–3 until the braid reaches the desired length.

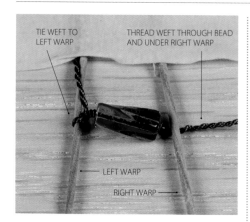

Loom-style weaving

1 For a loom-style weave, the basic set-up is to have two warp cords taped to the worktop at top and bottom, with a space between them for weaving. Next, take a finer thread to use as the weft. Usually this cord is tied to the left warp cord to begin. Add a bead on to the weft thread and pass the thread under the right warp cord.

2 Bring the weft around the right warp cord, moving towards the left, and thread it back through the bead and finally under the left warp cord.

3 Pull the weft cord tight, then repeat this process for the length of weave required.

ADDING FINDINGS

The following techniques are used throughout the project section to add findings to the jewellery, either as part of the construction or to finish off the pieces.

Crimps, cord ends and ribbon ends

All of these types of terminators use tension to hold the cords in place. They are designed to collapse in on themselves, or 'crimp', to do this. Once the terminator is in place, use chain-nose pliers to squeeze it on to the cord. Be careful, because if there is not enough pressure, the terminator will not hold the cord tightly enough and will fall off; if there is too much pressure, the cord may be cut. Once the terminator is crimped, pull on the cords to make sure that they are being held tightly enough.

SQUEEZE THE BOTTOM COILS TO SECURE COIL CORD END IN PLACE

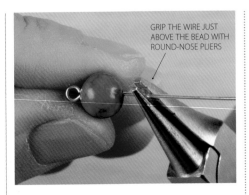

GRIP THE WIRE JUST ABOVE THE BEAD WITH ROUND-NOSE PLIERS

Simple wire loop

1 Wire loops are used when adding a bead to an eyepin or headpin. First, add the bead to the pin, and then bend the wire at a slight angle just above the bead. You can do this with your fingers or pliers. Then, grip the wire with round-nose pliers a little bit away from the bead. For a small loop, grip the wire closer to the end of the pliers; for a larger loop, grip the wire closer to the base of the pliers' nose.

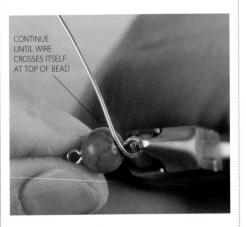

CONTINUE UNTIL WIRE CROSSES ITSELF AT TOP OF BEAD

3 Continue rolling the pliers around until the wire crosses itself right at the top of the bead. You may need to help the end of the wire the rest of the way around with your fingers.

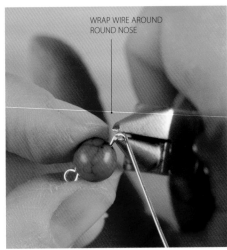

WRAP WIRE AROUND ROUND NOSE

2 Hold the bead in one hand and, using your wrist, roll the pliers towards the bead to wrap the wire around the nose of the pliers. If using pliers with only one round nose, make sure that you wrap the wire around this nose.

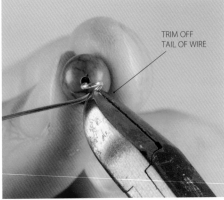

TRIM OFF TAIL OF WIRE

4 Remove the round-nose pliers and use a pair of wire cutters to trim the tail of the wire away. This new loop can now be opened and closed like a jump ring to attach it to a project.

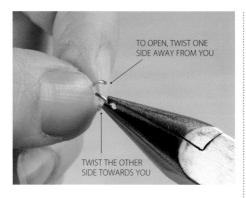

TO OPEN, TWIST ONE SIDE AWAY FROM YOU

TWIST THE OTHER SIDE TOWARDS YOU

MAKE SURE EDGES ALIGN WHEN CLOSING

Jump rings

1 To open a jump ring, hold the ring with the opening facing upwards. Grip one side with chain-nose pliers and the other with the tips of your fingers. Gently twist both sides in opposite directions, one towards you and the other away. Never pull the sides apart, because this will weaken the jump ring.

2 To close the jump ring, reverse the twisting motion to bring the ends back together, making sure that the ends line up. If the ring is too small to grasp between your fingertips, a second set of chain-nose pliers can be used to grip it.

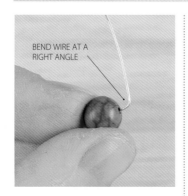

BEND WIRE AT A RIGHT ANGLE

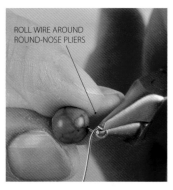

ROLL WIRE AROUND ROUND-NOSE PLIERS

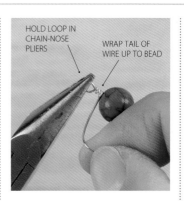

HOLD LOOP IN CHAIN-NOSE PLIERS

WRAP TAIL OF WIRE UP TO BEAD

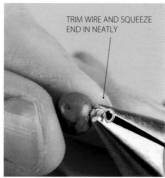

TRIM WIRE AND SQUEEZE END IN NEATLY

Wire-wrapped loop

1 A wire-wrapped loop is a wire loop with the tail end wrapped around the base of the loop for a secure connection. Once this loop is formed, it cannot be opened. First, add the bead to the pin, then bend the pin at a right angle a little above the top of the bead. You can do this with your fingers or by bending the wire back over the tip of a pair of chain-nose pliers.

2 Grip the wire with a pair of round-nose pliers, in the same way as for a simple wire loop. Holding the bead with your other hand, roll the pliers towards the bead to wrap the wire around the nose of the pliers. Help the end of the pin the rest of the way around with your fingertips so that it crosses itself right at the bend you made.

3 Switch to chain-nose pliers. Holding the loop with the pliers and the tail end of the pin with your fingers, wrap the tail around itself until it touches the bead.

4 Trim off the excess wire with wire cutters. Use chain-nose pliers to tuck the cut end into the twist so that there are no rough ends hanging out.

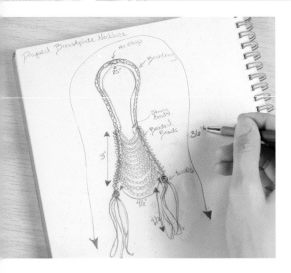

Sketching out your ideas will make your design become clearer in your mind, and will create a useful road map to help you bring it to life.

DESIGNING YOUR OWN JEWELLERY

Once you have mastered the basic leather jewellery techniques, you may wish to try your hand at designing your own projects. Here are some helpful hints and advice on bringing your creations to life.

Design checklist

To get started, here is a checklist of things to consider as you begin the design process.

STYLE

The very first thing to consider is what style you wish to design. Is it boho, modern, classic or romantic? Also take into account when the piece will be worn. Is it for everyday wear, going out or a special event? A good rule of thumb is that items meant for special events or for going out can be more elaborate than designs for casual wear. These two questions will help determine what type of materials to use and what colours will work best.

COLOURS

There are lots of 'rules' that say how to use colour, but in truth you can be as bold and bright or as subtle with colour as you like. The easiest way to choose is to pick one or two main colours and make the rest neutral or supporting colours that don't fight each other.

MEASUREMENTS

How big is the piece going to be? For necklaces, the length is important. A necklace must be at least 60cm (24in) long to fit over the head without a clasp. If it is shorter, some type of clasp or closure is needed.

For a bracelet, the length is determined by the size of the wrist. An average measurement for women is 18cm (7in), but this varies. The height of the bracelet will determine what findings you use to attach the clasp. For thin bracelets, simple cord ends work, but for wider cuff bracelets, you may need ribbon ends or a more creative solution.

Earrings can be as long or short as you want, and there are many different earwire and post options available. However, the weight of the earring is an important consideration. The heavier the earring, the more uncomfortable it is to wear over time.

MECHANICS

Consider the mechanics of the piece. How do you move from one section of the piece to another? If you are going to have multiple strands, they will need to come together somehow. Do you need a clasp for this design, and, if so, what type of connector or terminator would work best for attaching it? Also consider if you need glue for securing knots or attaching findings, or whether you can use a thread burner and crimp-on findings. If you are using glue, will a fast-drying or slow-drying type be more helpful to you?

MATERIALS

Assemble your materials list. Make a list of every item you will need for the design. Here is a handy cheat sheet to get you started:
• Leathers
• Silk or nylon threads and cords
• Beads
• Clasp
• Findings
• Tools

Sketching

Sketching out your design is a great way to go over all of the elements in the design checklist. You don't have to be a great sketch artist – the drawing only needs to make sense to you, and no one else has to see it, so don't stress too much about the details.

Make a simple diagram to show what goes where. This is just the road map of how one part flows into another. If you are missing something, drawing out the idea will help you work it out. Include measurements of different sections where necessary. Add notes on what things will be or could be. Add a little colour to your drawing, or add swatches or notes about the colour. Finally, use the sketch to double-check your list of materials.

Style: Boho – spirited and flowing
Colours: Earth tones, rust red, turquoise, soft brown, brass
Types of jewellery: Long necklaces and earrings, wrap bracelets
Techniques: Tassels, braiding, knotting

Style: Modern – sleek and simple
Colours: Bright colours, red, blue, black, dark brown, silver
Types of jewellery: Shorter necklaces and earrings, cuff bracelets
Techniques: Braiding, weaving, macramé

Style: Classic – simple and more conservative
Colours: Neutral tones, pink, ivory, navy, gold, pearls
Types of jewellery: Shorter necklaces and earrings, simple bracelets
Techniques: Knotting, braiding, weaving

Style: Romantic – layers and soft textures
Colours: Soft colours, pale blue, pink, cream, pearls, gemstones
Types of jewellery: Longer necklaces and earrings, simple bracelets
Techniques: Knotting, braiding, multiple strands

Choosing materials

Your choice of materials will depend on both personal preference and practical functionality.

BEADS

Whether you choose a pearl over a gemstone or a wooden bead over a glass bead will depend on your own personal design tastes. There are so many options for every size, shape, colour and price that the choices are limitless, but here are a few things to keep in mind when you are shopping.

• Which direction is the hole drilled, and is there even a hole? The way the hole is drilled will determine how the bead will be used. Some beads have holes that go straight through the middle, while others are drilled at the top so they can hang like a pendant. Some beads don't have any hole at all, so it is important to make a note of this.

• Next, how large are the holes? Gemstones and pearls tend to have smaller holes than other types of beads. Wood, horn and metal beads tend to have larger holes. Beads made from man-made

A cord such as 1mm round leather (above) is ideal for projects that require tight knots, whereas rawhide lace (above right) does not knot easily and is better suited to braided projects.

materials, such as glass, plastic and metal, tend to have consistent hole sizes from bead to bead. It is essential to check that any beads you buy will fit on the cord you have chosen before you start the project.

• Finally, how heavy are the beads? Remember that you will be wearing this jewellery, so consider if the weight of the beads might be uncomfortable over time. This is especially important when it comes to earrings. Also, mixing and matching lightweight and heavy beads can distort the way the design hangs. If you do choose to use a lighter bead with a heavier bead, make sure that you use the weight difference to your advantage.

CORDS

Here are some things to consider when it comes to choosing the right cord for the job.

• How big are the beads' holes? Reaming can only make the holes slightly larger and is mostly used to even out the inside of the bead, so test the beads to make sure they fit on the cord you have chosen.

• Are the beads large or heavy? The heavier or larger the bead, the thicker and stronger the cord should be to support the beads, both in weight and visually.

• One last thing to consider is whether the cord is good for the technique you are going to use. Some cords knot better than others, and other cords are better for braiding than others. It is helpful to make a sample swatch of the technique with your actual materials to test whether the design will work.

FINDINGS

The hardware of the piece should not be an afterthought. Sometimes a great clasp can make or break the finished project. At times you want the findings to stand out, but at others you want them to fade into the background. Size also matters. If the clasp is too big, it may look out of place on the finished design. Conversely, if the clasp is too small, it may be difficult to operate. The weight of the finished piece may also tell you what type of clasp to use. If the finished necklace or bracelet is really lightweight, a clasp that closes securely, such as a lobster clasp, might be a better choice than a hook-and-eye clasp.

When it comes to terminators like cord and ribbon ends, it is very important to make sure that they will fit the finished piece. Also, does the terminator allow the design to lie naturally the way you envisioned? And, finally, are there any other findings you will need, and will they fit the size, shape and design of the project?

These are both 4mm round beads, but the gemstones (above) have small holes, while the metal beads (left) have larger holes.

A large hook clasp (above left) is suitable for a bold design, whereas a simple button (below left) provides a more subtle closure.

How to measure yourself

Measuring yourself or the person you are making the jewellery for is important to ensure that the finished design will both fit properly and be flattering when worn. This will also help you to customise the projects in this book to your size. Here are a few tips to help you measure.

· **Necklace** – use a tape measure and place it around your neck as if it were a necklace to get the measurement.

· **Bracelet** – measure your wrist just below the wrist bone. Add at least 13mm (½in) to the measurement to allow the bracelet to move and clasp easily.

· **Bangle** – tuck your thumb behind your fingers as if you were putting on a bangle and measure around your knuckles to get the total measurement.

· **Earrings** – measure from your actual piercing, or in the case of clip-ons from where the earring will sit on your earlobe, and measure straight down. Subtract the length of the earwire from this measurement to get the length you have to work with.

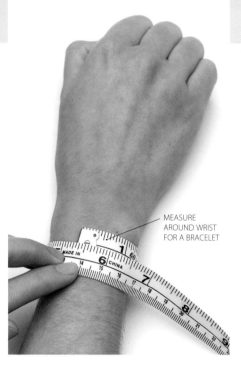

MEASURE AROUND WRIST FOR A BRACELET

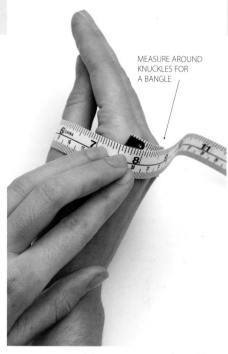

MEASURE AROUND KNUCKLES FOR A BANGLE

Calculating quantities

It is hard to estimate how much cord or beads are needed, but it is always better to have too much than too little.

CORD LENGTHS

· **Plain strung cords** – always give yourself an extra 5–10cm (2–4in) wiggle room to work with.

· **Macramé or simple knotting** – multiply the finished measurement by 3 to get the amount needed per cord. Then, multiply that number by the number of cords in the macramé to get the total length of cord needed for the project. For example:

(Length of finished macramé) x 3 = (length of cord) x (number of cords) = (total length for project)

· **Braids** – there is a similar formula for a braid, but instead of multiplying by 3 you should multiply the finished measurement by 2 to get the length of each cord in the braid. Then, multiply that length by the number of cords in the braid to get the total amount of cord needed for the project. For example:

(Length of finished braid) x 2 = (length of cord) x (number of cords) = (total length for project)

NUMBER OF BEADS

· **Straight beaded section** – take the final measurement and divide it by the size of the beads. For example:

(Length of finished beading) ÷ (size of beads) = (number of beads for beaded section)

· **Knotted, braided and macramé beading** – for projects that involve knotting between beads, braiding or macramé, this will give you more beads than you need, but it is a place to start. You can also do a small sample swatch of the technique you will use with the beads and the cord and measure the length between beads to find a more accurate number. For example:

(Length of finished beading) ÷ [(size of bead) + (space between beads)] = (number of beads for beaded section)

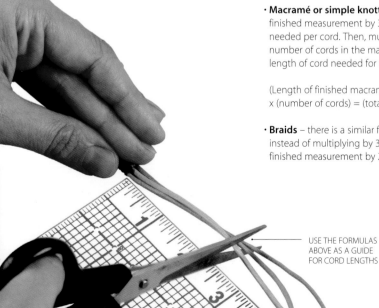

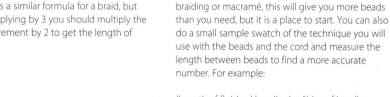

USE THE FORMULAS ABOVE AS A GUIDE FOR CORD LENGTHS

CHAPTER 2

THE PROJECTS

This chapter features more than 30 projects for making leather and bead jewellery, from earrings and bracelets to pendants and necklaces. The projects are arranged by technique, beginning with a section of simple stringing and knotting projects that will help you build up the skills you will need for making the more complex designs that follow. The last few projects mix jewellery-making techniques and utilise all of the skills learned from previous projects.

BASICS   WEAVE   MACRAMÉ   MIXED

THE BASICS

The simpler techniques are always a good place to start, but that does not mean that the finished project cannot be a stylish piece of jewellery. These first few projects use basic jewellery-making methods to create simple but beautiful pieces. This includes stringing and knotting techniques, as well as how to finish jewellery and use findings. Some of the projects are quick and easy, while others will challenge your newly acquired skills and will prepare you for the projects ahead.

SUN DANCER NECKLACE

A bib necklace is a great way to dress up a simple outfit. In this project you will learn how to use findings to create transitions within a piece of jewellery. Three strands of large, attention-grabbing beads at the front change over to soft deer-hide leather lace at the back using decorative metal links. The necklace is finished with an easy-to-use button clasp at the back.

Materials

Two 60cm (24in) lengths of 3mm flat deer-hide leather lace

Ten 10mm faceted round beads

Thirteen 10mm smooth round beads

Twenty-nine 17 x 7mm top-drilled spike beads

One 1.8m (2yd) card of #4 silk thread with needle

Two 20mm round metal links

One 13mm (½in) button with shank

One 6mm jump ring

Six 2mm round metal crimps

Toolkit

Ruler

Scissors

Chain-nose pliers

Glue

Size
53cm (21in) inside;
58cm (23in) outside

Spike beads

Button

Metal links

Smooth beads

Crimps

Silk thread

Faceted beads

Flat leather lace

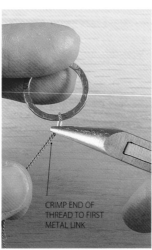

CRIMP END OF THREAD TO FIRST METAL LINK

STRING THE FACETED BEADS

CRIMP TO SECOND METAL LINK AFTER BEADS

1 Use chain-nose pliers to attach the end of the silk thread to one metal link with a crimp. String all ten faceted round beads on to the silk. Make sure that you leave enough slack so that the beads drape nicely when held up but do not show any loose silk thread. Crimp the other end to the second metal link.

THREE STRANDS OF BEADS

2 Repeat step 1 with all of the smooth round beads and then with all of the spike beads so that three individual strands hang from the two metal links. Be careful not to twist the strands while crimping. Each strand should lie nicely inside the one below it.

ATTACH LEATHER
WITH A LARK'S
HEAD KNOT

GLUE KNOT
SECURELY

OVERHAND KNOT

3 Fold one length of leather lace in half so that the smooth sides are both facing you. The looped end will not lie flat. Form a lark's head knot by placing the looped end over one of the metal links with the smooth side facing up, then pulling the ends of the lace up through the link and loop. Repeat with the second lace and link. If the leather does not twist, only the smooth surface should be facing you in the knot.

4 Attach the jump ring to the shank button. Take the ends of the leather lace on the right side of the necklace and thread them through the jump ring. Position the button so that it is 19cm (7½in) from the metal link and tie an overhand knot, catching the button in the knot. Trim excess leather away and glue the knot to secure.

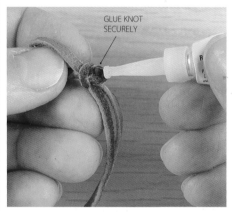

GLUE KNOT
SECURELY

KEEP SMOOTH
SIDE OF LEATHER
FACING UPWARDS

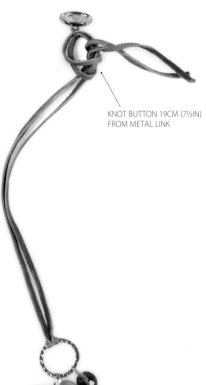

KNOT BUTTON 19CM (7½IN)
FROM METAL LINK

5 To form a button loop with the leather lace on the left side of the necklace, measure 20cm (8in) from the metal link and fold the lace over on itself at this point. Make an overhand knot around the loop with the tail ends, 1.5cm (⁵⁄₈in) away from the folded edge. Trim excess leather away and glue the knot to secure.

POSITION KNOT 1.5CM (⁵⁄₈IN)
FROM FOLDED END OF
BUTTON LOOP

WILD HEART BRACELET

Multi-strand bracelets add a feeling of luxury to any style, but that does not mean they have to be complicated to make. Just a few simple supplies and tools are needed for this dramatic bracelet.

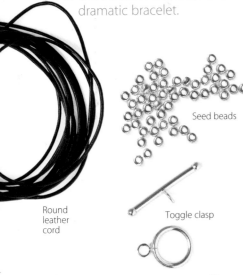

Round leather cord

Seed beads

Toggle clasp

Jump rings

Size
19cm (7½in) long
plus 2.5cm (1in) tassel

Materials

Three 60cm (24in) lengths of 0.5mm round leather cord

One-hundred-and-eight #6 metallic seed beads

One 12mm toggle clasp

Two 6mm jump rings

Toolkit

Ruler

Scissors

Chain-nose pliers

Tape

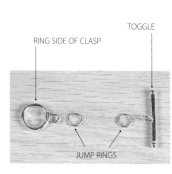

RING SIDE OF CLASP

TOGGLE

JUMP RINGS

LARK'S HEAD KNOT

EACH KNOT SHOULD FACE IN SAME DIRECTION

1 Attach a jump ring to each end of the toggle clasp, making sure that they are closed tightly.

2 Fold one piece of leather cord in half and tie it with a lark's head knot to the jump ring at the ring end of the clasp (see page 21). Repeat with the other two leather cords, making sure that all three lark's head knots face the same direction.

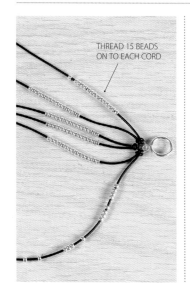

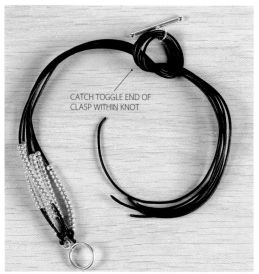

THREAD 15 BEADS ON TO EACH CORD

CATCH TOGGLE END OF CLASP WITHIN KNOT

3 BEADS PER CORD FOR THE TASSEL

SECURE BEADS WITH OVERHAND KNOT, THEN TRIM CORD

3 String 15 beads on to each of the six strands of leather. If the beads are loose on the cord, place a piece of tape over the end of the cord like a flag. This will keep the beads from sliding off as you work.

4 Thread all six strands through the jump ring at the toggle end of the clasp. Make an overhand knot, catching the jump ring in the knot 18cm (7in) from the ring end of the clasp.

5 For the tassel, string three beads on to each loose end of leather cord and tie an overhand knot about 2.5cm (1in) from the toggle. Trim each cord to 6mm (¼in) away from the knot.

STARLET BRACELET

Knotting between beads is a classic jewellery-making technique. Although it is usually done in silk, it adds a refined look to leather jewellery as well. In this project you will learn the technique of using tweezers to guide knots to the right place, and how to finish off the bracelet with a sliding clasp in a contrasting colour.

Rondelle beads

Round leather cord

Metal beads

Nylon cord

Size

15–21.5cm (6–8½in) circumference

Materials

One 76cm (30in) length of 1mm round leather cord

Twenty-four 7 x 5mm faceted rondelle beads

Six 4mm round metal beads

One 38cm (15in) length of #14 or 1mm nylon cord

Toolkit

Ruler

Scissors

Tweezers

Thread burner

USE TWEEZERS
TO GUIDE KNOT
UP TO BEADS

1 Make an overhand knot at one end of the leather cord and slide three round metal beads up to the knot. Make an overhand knot, using tweezers to direct the knot right against the beads. Do this by slipping the tweezers through the knot and grasping the cord where you want the knot to land.

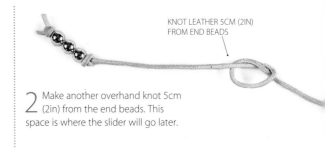

KNOT LEATHER 5CM (2IN)
FROM END BEADS

2 Make another overhand knot 5cm (2in) from the end beads. This space is where the slider will go later.

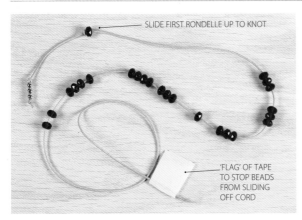

SLIDE FIRST RONDELLE UP TO KNOT

'FLAG' OF TAPE
TO STOP BEADS
FROM SLIDING
OFF CORD

3 String all 24 faceted rondelle beads on to the cord and place a piece of tape over the end of the cord like a flag to keep the beads from sliding off. Slide the first bead up to the last knot made.

4 Make another overhand knot, using the tweezers to make sure the knot lands right against the bead. Repeat this process for all of the rondelle beads. Remove the tape from the end. The finished knotted section should measure 18cm (7in) from first to last knot.

PLACE A KNOT
ON OTHER SIDE
OF BEAD

5CM (2IN) PLAIN
SECTIONS FOR
SLIDER CLASP

ABOUT 7 WRAPS

KNOT ENDS
TOGETHER

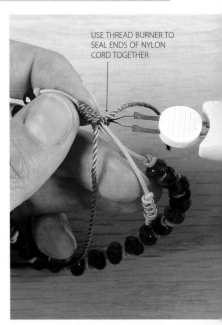

USE THREAD BURNER TO
SEAL ENDS OF NYLON
CORD TOGETHER

5 Make another overhand knot 5cm (2in) from the last knot and string the last three metal beads on. Make one last overhand knot against the last bead. Trim the excess at both ends to 6mm (¼in). This section is a mirror image of step 1.

6 Make a circle with the knotted bracelet, overlapping the two plain 5cm (2in) sections. Take the nylon cord, fold over a 5cm (2in) long section at one end and place it along the overlapped plain leather sections. With the long end, wrap the nylon cord around the leather about seven times. Tie a simple knot with both ends of the nylon cord. Test the slider by pulling gently on the leather ends to make sure that they move smoothly. You may need to adjust the tightness of the slider accordingly. Once you are happy with the slider, use a thread burner to seal the ends together, taking care not to burn the leather, and then trim away excess nylon cord.

Metal charms

GOLDEN SUMMER LARIAT

A lariat may be a simple necklace, but it has endless possibilities, depending on how you wear it. In this project you will practise simple overhand knots to attach beads and charms to leather cord. The finished lariat can be worn as a necklace or a wrap bracelet.

Glass beads

Materials

One 1.8m (2yd) length of 0.5mm round leather cord

Twelve 19 x 5mm metal charms

Thirty 4mm round glass beads

Twelve 4 x 3mm metal tube beads

Toolkit

Ruler

Scissors

Tape

Tube beads

Round leather cord

Size
56cm (22in) long, doubled

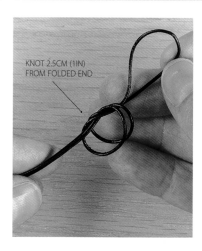

KNOT 2.5CM (1IN)
FROM FOLDED END

1 Fold the leather cord in half and tie an overhand knot about 2.5cm (1in) from the folded end. This will form the loop that the ends will pass through when the lariat is worn.

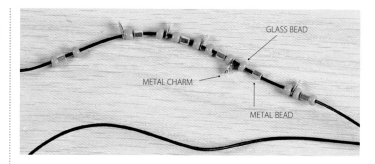

GLASS BEAD

METAL CHARM

METAL BEAD

2 Beginning on one side, string twelve glass beads, six metal tube beads and five metal charms in the following pattern: 1 glass bead, 1 metal bead, 1 glass bead, 1 metal charm. Repeat until you have strung all of the beads, then place a piece of tape over the end of the leather like a flag to keep the beads from falling off.

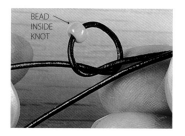

BEAD INSIDE KNOT

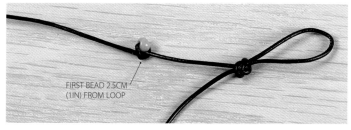

FIRST BEAD 2.5CM (1IN) FROM LOOP

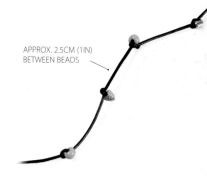

APPROX. 2.5CM (1IN) BETWEEN BEADS

3 Slide the first glass bead up the leather to about 2.5cm (1in) from the loop. Make an overhand knot with the bead inside the loop, so that the bead is secured in place and appears to hang off the leather cord. Continue with the second bead in line, positioning it roughly 2.5cm

(1in) from the first. Continue knotting until you have knotted all of the beads. Don't worry if the placement of the beads is not exact; having slightly varied spacing adds to the free-form style of the piece. The finished knotted section should measure 60cm (24in) from the loop to the last bead.

METAL CHARM INSIDE KNOT

4 For the finished end, string three glass beads and one metal charm on to the end of the lariat. Then, 5cm (2in) from the last knotted bead, make an overhand knot with the charm inside the loop to secure the final beads on to the leather. Pull the last knot tight and trim excess 6mm (¼in) away from the knot. The three glass beads will remain loose to slide on the leather cord.

5 Repeat steps 2–4 on the other side of the leather cord to complete.

MERMAID CUFF

Making this bracelet will teach you how to make beads hang like charms on leather using headpins. The bracelet is formed in a double-wrap style, with sliding barrel knots to make it adjustable. Gemstone nuggets cluster and slide on the leather like a charm bracelet.

Materials

One 60cm (24in) length of 3mm flat deer-hide leather lace

Twenty-four gemstone chips in different colours

Twenty-four 5cm (2in) long 24-gauge headpins

Toolkit

Ruler

Scissors

Round-nose pliers

Chain-nose pliers

Wire cutters

Size

15–20cm (6–8in) circumference

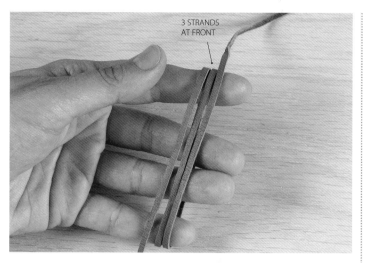

3 STRANDS AT FRONT

1 Wrap the leather lace around four of your fingers twice. The leather will overlap at the front so that three strands lie next to each other. The resulting circle should measure 9cm (3½in) when laid flat.

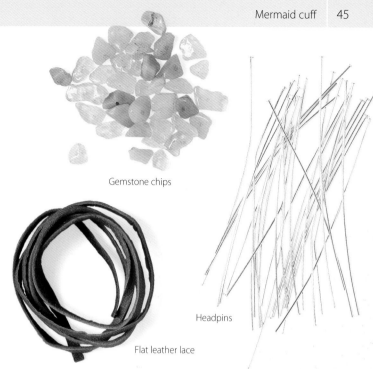

Gemstone chips

Flat leather lace

Headpins

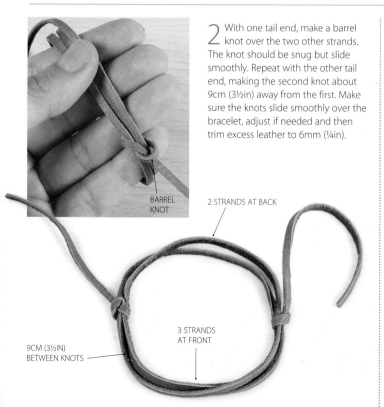

BARREL KNOT

2 STRANDS AT BACK

3 STRANDS AT FRONT

9CM (3½IN) BETWEEN KNOTS

2 With one tail end, make a barrel knot over the two other strands. The knot should be snug but slide smoothly. Repeat with the other tail end, making the second knot about 9cm (3½in) away from the first. Make sure the knots slide smoothly over the bracelet, adjust if needed and then trim excess leather to 6mm (¼in).

FORM WIRE LOOP

3 Put each gemstone chip on to a headpin and use round-nose pliers to make a simple wire loop roughly 6mm (¼in) in diameter (see page 26). Trim off extra wire using wire cutters.

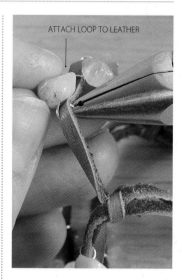

ATTACH LOOP TO LEATHER

4 Using chain-nose pliers, open each loop like you would open a jump ring and attach each pin to the leather. Distribute the stones around the strands of leather, with half at the front and half at the back of the bracelet.

BOHO TASSEL EARRINGS

These fun fringe earrings dance as you move. The fringe is embellished with sparkling beads that catch the light. The fringe is made like a tassel and topped with a metal cone to give the earrings a refined look.

Round leather cord

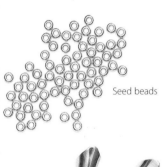

Seed beads

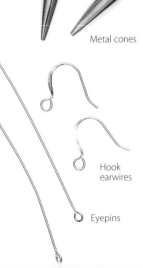

Metal cones

Hook earwires

Eyepins

Materials

Eight 25cm (10in) lengths of 0.5mm round leather cord

Two 30cm (12in) lengths of 0.5mm round leather cord

Sixty #6 metallic seed beads

Two 12 x 8mm metal cones

Two 7.5cm (3in) long 21-gauge eyepins

Two hook earwires

Toolkit

Ruler

Scissors

Round-nose pliers

Chain-nose pliers

Wire cutters

Size

10cm (4in) long

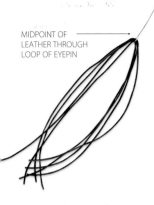

MIDPOINT OF LEATHER THROUGH LOOP OF EYEPIN

1 Open the loop of one eyepin like a jump ring and place four 25cm (10in) lengths of round leather cord through the open loop so that the loop is at the midpoint of the cords. Close the loop carefully using chain-nose pliers.

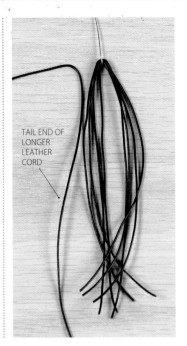

TAIL END OF LONGER LEATHER CORD

WRAP LONGER CORD AROUND THE OTHERS

TAIL END OF WRAPPING CORD

DOUBLE KNOT

2 Line up one 30cm (12in) length of leather cord with the cords inside the eyepin, allowing the tail end to hang down as part of the tassel for the moment. Wrap the cord around the others three times just under the eyepin, making sure that you capture all the cords in the eyepin and the tail end of the wrapping cord inside. Tie a double overhand knot with the ends of the wrapping cord to secure.

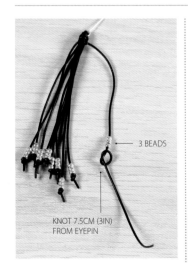

3 BEADS

KNOT 7.5CM (3IN) FROM EYEPIN

3 Add three beads to each cord (including wrapping cord) and tie an overhand knot 7.5cm (3in) from the eyepin loop. Trim the excess to 6mm (¼in) from the knot.

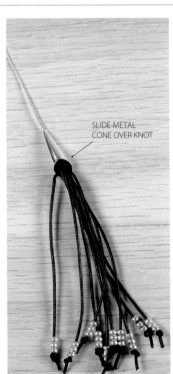

SLIDE METAL CONE OVER KNOT

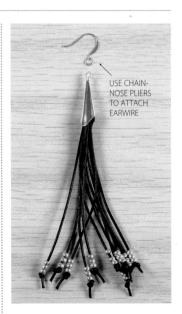

FORM LOOP WITH EYEPIN WIRE AT TOP OF CONE

4 Slide a metal cone on to the eyepin so that the wider end covers the eyepin loop and the top of the cords. Use round-nose pliers to form a simple wire loop at the top of the cone, then cut off excess wire with wire cutters (see page 26).

USE CHAIN-NOSE PLIERS TO ATTACH EARWIRE

5 Attach the earwire and repeat all steps to make the second earring.

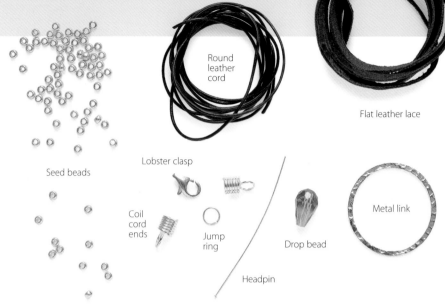

Round leather cord

Flat leather lace

Seed beads

Lobster clasp

Coil cord ends

Jump ring

Metal link

Drop bead

Headpin

DREAMCATCHER NECKLACE

This dreamy necklace is inspired by the dreamcatchers that are hung in the hope of catching bad dreams and only letting good dreams through. A glittering crystal hangs suspended in a round metal link, with beaded fringe adorning it.

Materials

One 77.5cm (30½in) length of 3mm flat leather lace

Seven 23cm (9in) lengths of 0.5mm round leather cord

One 12 x 7mm faceted crystal drop bead drilled top to bottom

Seventy #6 metallic seed beads

One 30mm round metal link

One 5cm (2in) long 24-gauge headpin

Two coil cord ends

One 10 x 6mm lobster clasp

One 6mm jump ring

Toolkit

Ruler

Scissors

Round-nose pliers

Chain-nose pliers

Wire cutters

Size
76cm (30in) long with 10cm (4in) pendant

SECURE CRYSTAL DROP TO METAL LINK WITH WIRE-WRAPPED LOOP

CATCH CRYSTAL WITHIN LARK'S HEAD KNOT

JOIN ROUND CORDS WITH LARK'S HEAD KNOTS

1 Slide the crystal drop on to the headpin. Loop the headpin around the metal link, then wrap the end of the headpin around the base of the loop just above the crystal drop (see page 27). Trim away excess wire.

2 Position the crystal drop so that it is at the top of the metal link and hanging inside the circle. Using the flat leather lace, make a lark's head knot over the top of the metal link, capturing the crystal drop between the two sides of the knot (see page 21).

3 Fold each round leather cord in half and use lark's head knots to attach them to the bottom of the metal link. Make sure all knots are facing the same way and the cords are even. Pull each knot tight to secure in place.

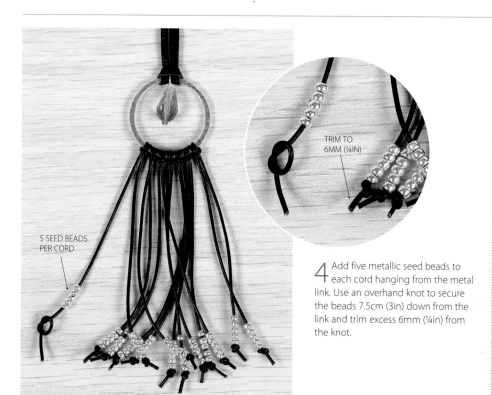

5 SEED BEADS PER CORD

TRIM TO 6MM (¼IN)

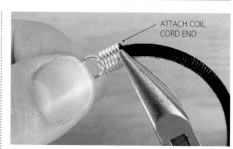

ATTACH COIL CORD END

5 Attach a coil cord end to each end of the flat lace at the back. Use chain-nose pliers to squeeze the last two coils of the cord end around the leather.

4 Add five metallic seed beads to each cord hanging from the metal link. Use an overhand knot to secure the beads 7.5cm (3in) down from the link and trim excess 6mm (¼in) from the knot.

6 On the right side of the necklace, open the loop of the coil cord end and attach the lobster clasp. On the left side, attach a jump ring.

LOBSTER CLASP   JUMP RING

Materials

One 2.6m (8½ft) length of 1.5mm round leather cord

Eight 23cm (9in) lengths of 3mm flat deer-hide leather lace

Fifty 10mm natural wood rounded triangle beads

Ten 10mm metallic wood rounded triangle beads

One 4 x 4mm square metal crimp

Toolkit

Ruler

Scissors

Tweezers

Chain-nose pliers

Flat leather lace

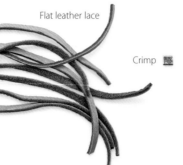

Natural wood beads

Metallic wood beads

Crimp

Round leather cord

JOURNEY TASSEL NECKLACE

Size
86cm (34in) long
plus 9cm (3½in) tassel

Tassel necklaces are a fun, fashionable accessory. Here, a soft leather tassel hangs beautifully from a knotted string of natural and metallic wooden beads. This project teaches you how to clean-finish a piece of jewellery, where the cord ends are hidden and no findings are visible. You will also practise how to knot between beads and make tassels.

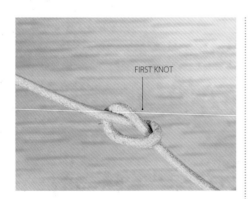

FIRST KNOT

1 Make an overhand knot 10cm (4in) from one end of the round leather cord. String all 60 beads in the following pattern: 3 metallic, 10 natural, 1 metallic, 10 natural, 1 metallic, 10 natural, 1 metallic, 10 natural, 1 metallic, 10 natural, 3 metallic.

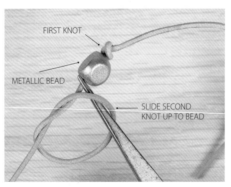

FIRST KNOT

METALLIC BEAD

SLIDE SECOND KNOT UP TO BEAD

2 Slide the first bead up to the first knot. Make another overhand knot and use tweezers to direct the knot up against the bead. Repeat this step for all 60 beads. Coil the long end of the leather for the first few knots to make working with it more manageable. Trim each end of the beaded cord 10cm (4in) from the first and last knots.

TRIM ENDS TO 10CM (4IN)

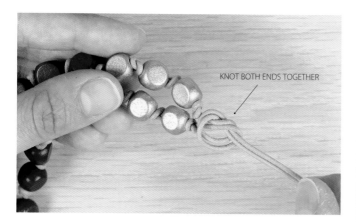

KNOT BOTH ENDS TOGETHER

7 FLAT DEER-HIDE LACES ARE THREADED THROUGH HERE IN STEP 4

METAL CRIMP

3 Tie one last overhand knot using both ends of cord and pull tight next to the end knots. Slide a metal crimp on to both ends and position it 4cm (1½in) from the knot, but do not crimp.

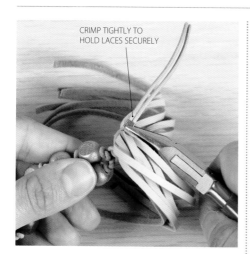

CRIMP TIGHTLY TO HOLD LACES SECURELY

TIE LAST LACE AROUND TASSEL TO HIDE CRIMP

4 Line up seven lengths of flat deer-hide lace and thread them through the opening between the final knot and the metal crimp. Make sure the laces are even on both sides. Slide the metal crimp up to the leather laces and crimp tightly. Trim away extra round leather cord just below the crimp.

5 Adjust the laces to cover the metal crimp, making sure the flat leather side of the lace is facing out. Line up the final length of deer-hide leather with the others, allowing the tail end to hang down as part of the tassel for the moment. Wrap the cord around the others four times at the top of the tassel, making sure that you capture all the cords and the tail end of the wrapping cord inside. Tie a double overhand knot with the ends of the wrapping cord to secure.

MOONBEAM BANGLE

Bangles are clean-finished bracelets – a continuous piece with no beginning or end point and no findings visible – that are large enough to slide over your hand. This means there is no need for a clasp. For this bracelet, you will create a clean-finished bangle with twisted interlinking loops adorned with colourful strands of beads at the front.

Round leather cord

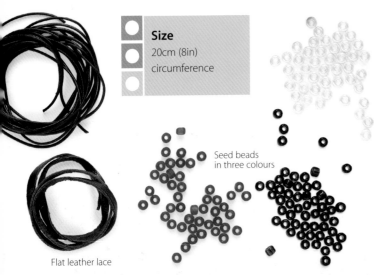

Size
20cm (8in) circumference

Seed beads in three colours

Flat leather lace

Materials

Six 30cm (12in) lengths of 1mm round leather cord

One 46cm (18in) length of 3mm flat leather lace

Three colours of #6 seed beads

Toolkit

Ruler

Scissors

Bradawl

Tape

Glue

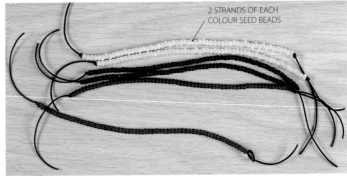

2 STRANDS OF EACH COLOUR SEED BEADS

1 Take one length of round leather cord and make a knot 6cm (2½in) from the end. String 16.5cm (6½in) of one colour seed beads and knot the end. The beads should lie nicely and not be crunched. Repeat this step to create two strands of each seed bead colour, for a total of six strands.

TWIST 3 CORDS OF DIFFERENT COLOUR SEED BEADS TOGETHER

2 Line up three of the cords, one of each colour seed beads, and begin twisting them together until they twist back on themselves. This will form a loop at the end. Tape the ends together to hold the twist.

TAPE ENDS TOGETHER

LOOPED END

TWIST REMAINING 3 CORDS, LINKED TOGETHER THROUGH LOOP OF FIRST GROUP

3 Line up the remaining three beaded cords and begin twisting them as before, but thread the ends through the loop of the first twisted group before allowing them to collapse back on themselves. This will link the two twists together. Tape the ends together to hold the twist.

OVERLAP AND TAPE THE ENDS

4 Make a circle with the linked twists that is 20cm (8in) in diameter. There should be a 5cm (2in) overlap at the back. Wrap a piece of tape around all cords at the centre of the overlap. Trim any loose ends flush with the tape.

WRAP FLAT LACE AROUND GLUED JOIN

5 Place glue all along the overlapping section at the back. Fold the flat leather lace 3cm (1¼in) from one end and lay the short end alongside the taped section of the beaded circle. With the long end, coil the lace around the bundle, working towards the loop until it is at least 5cm (2in) long and covers all of the loose ends. Trim the end of the lace to 13mm (½in) and use a bradawl to tuck the tail into the coil. Press firmly on the coil to adhere the glue. Wipe away any glue that seeps between the coils before it dries.

BRAIDING AND WEAVING

Braiding and weaving are two related techniques that are traditionally used to make beaded leather jewellery. Beads can be threaded on to cords in a braid, or beaded strands can be braided alongside leather cords. Weaving allows you to create a textile of leather and beads that can be used in a variety of ways, from cuff bracelets to pendants. With a little imagination, the possibilities are endless. The first few projects focus on braiding and how to incorporate beads. The later projects explore different methods of weaving to create unique pieces of jewellery.

GOLD-DIPPED COLLAR

Feel like Cleopatra wearing this necklace that looks like it has been dipped in gold. The beads are incorporated into the multi-strand braid to create a scalloped edge.

Materials

Nine 81cm (32in) lengths of 1mm round leather cord

Sixty-four 4mm round metal beads

Two 10 x 5mm ribbon ends

One 22 x 10mm S-hook clasp

Two 6mm jump rings

Toolkit

Ruler

Scissors

Chain-nose pliers

Tape

Glue

Size

51cm (20in) long

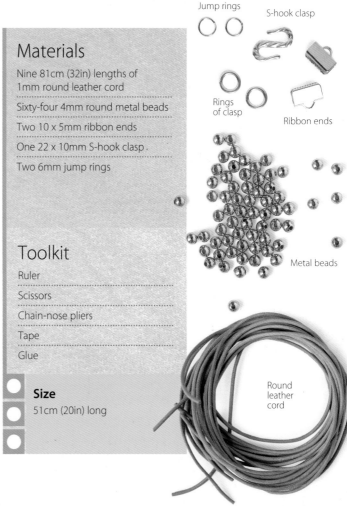

Jump rings

S-hook clasp

Rings of clasp

Ribbon ends

Metal beads

Round leather cord

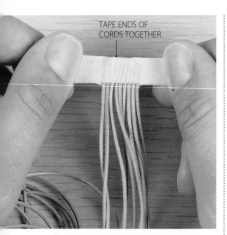

TAPE ENDS OF
CORDS TOGETHER

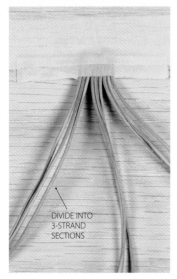

DIVIDE INTO
3-STRAND
SECTIONS

BRAID FOR
19CM (7½IN)

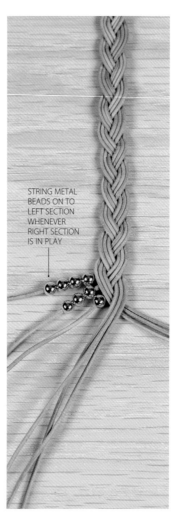

STRING METAL
BEADS ON TO
LEFT SECTION
WHENEVER
RIGHT SECTION
IS IN PLAY

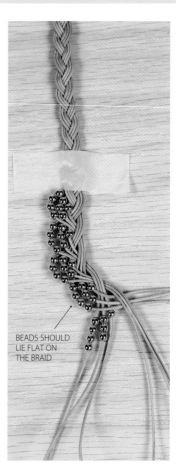

BEADS SHOULD
LIE FLAT ON
THE BRAID

12.5CM (5IN) OF
BEADED BRAID

1 Prepare the leather cord for braiding by creating a binding of tape at one end. Lay out the ends of each strand side by side on a piece of tape. Then fold the edge of the tape over, sealing the cord ends inside. Tape the bound edge down to the worktop. Divide the cords into three sections of three cords each.

2 Begin to braid a simple three-strand braid. Make sure while braiding that you keep the cords in each of the sections flat. Continue until the braid is 19cm (7½in) long and the next section in play is on the right side. You may find it helpful to tape down the braid at the end of this plain section.

3 On the left-hand section of three cords, string four metal beads on to the left cord, three on to the middle cord and one on to the right cord. Braid as before, making sure that you pull the cords so the beads lie flat. Repeat this for 12.5cm (5in), adding beads to the left-hand section whenever each right section comes into play. Again, you may find it helpful to tape the braid down at the end of this beaded section.

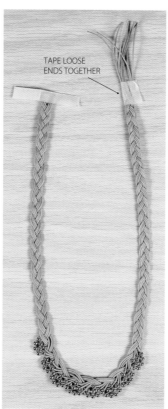

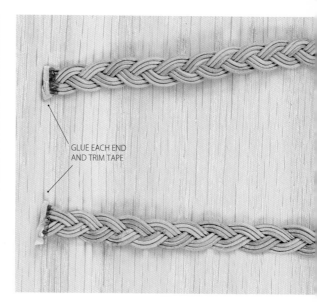

4 Braid without beads as in step 2, making sure that the beaded section continues to lie flat. This plain section should measure 19cm (7½in).

BRAID WITHOUT BEADS FOR 19CM (7½IN)

TAPE LOOSE ENDS TOGETHER

GLUE EACH END AND TRIM TAPE

5 Tape down the loose strands and apply a ribbon of glue at each end just below the tape. Allow the glue to dry until it is tacky and holds its shape, then cut the ends of the braid, leaving a small sliver of tape at each end. This will create a clean edge to insert into the ribbon ends.

ATTACH RIBBON END TO EACH END OF BRAID

6 Using chain-nose pliers, crimp a ribbon end over the glued tape at each end of the braid, then attach the ribbon ends to the S-hook clasp using jump rings.

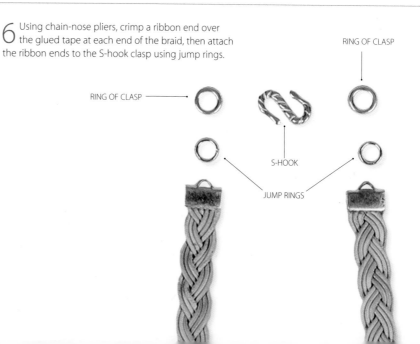

RING OF CLASP

RING OF CLASP

S-HOOK

JUMP RINGS

CANYON WRAP BRACELET

A fishtail braid is a simple braid that can be made with many strands and forms a unique chevron pattern. Accentuate the pattern by using contrasting colours and beads in this double-wrap bracelet.

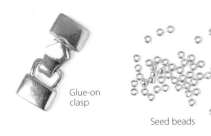

Glue-on clasp

Seed beads

Silk thread

Flat leather laces in two colours

Size

38cm (15in) long

Materials

Two 51cm (20in) lengths of 3mm flat brown rawhide lace

Two 51cm (20in) lengths of 3mm flat rawhide lace in contrasting colour

One 1.8m (2yd) card of #6 silk thread with needle

#6 metallic seed beads

One 13 x 30mm glue-on clasp

Toolkit

Ruler

Scissors

Tape

Glue

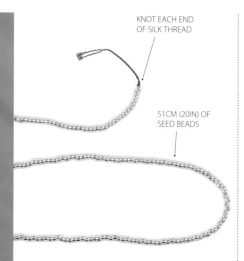

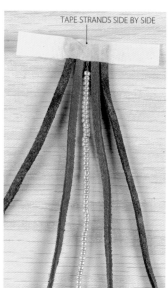

KNOT EACH END
OF SILK THREAD

51CM (20IN) OF
SEED BEADS

TAPE STRANDS SIDE BY SIDE

MOVE FAR LEFT
STRAND TO CENTRE

MOVE FAR RIGHT
STRAND TO CENTRE

BRAID FOR 36CM (14IN)

1 String a 51cm (20in) length of seed beads on to the silk thread and secure each end with an overhand knot.

2 Line up all the strands in the following order: 1 brown lace, 1 contrast lace, 1 beaded strand, 1 contrast lace, 1 brown lace. This arrangement will create a chevron pattern. Bind the edge with tape and then tape it down to the worktop.

3 Separate the strands into two sections, with two strands on the left and three strands on the right. Take the far left strand, overlap the other left strand and move it to the inside of the right section. Take the far right strand and do the same, moving it to the inside of the left section. Repeat these two moves, taking care not to twist the leather. As the braid progresses, a chevron pattern will emerge. Continue until the braid is 36cm (14in) long. Remove any extra beads and tie off the end of the beaded strand. When finished, tape down the end of the braid.

TRIM EACH END, LEAVING
A SLIVER OF TAPE

APPLY GLUE
AT EACH END

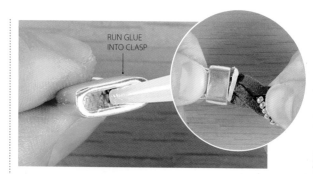

RUN GLUE
INTO CLASP

4 Run a ribbon of glue along each end of the braid just below the tape. When the glue is dry but still tacky, cut off the taped ends, leaving only a small sliver of tape behind.

5 Run glue inside the clasp. Insert the ends of the braid into each end of the clasp. Wipe away any excess glue that squeezes out when the braid is inserted and then allow to dry.

Focal stone

Flat leather laces

Size

18cm (7in) long

ARIZONA FRINGE CUFF

Using large beads is a great way to add a lot of drama to a piece of jewellery. This cuff bracelet features a 35mm focal stone on a six-strand braided cuff and is finished off with some fringe at the clasp for a bit of fun.

Ribbon ends

Hook-and-eye clasp

Eyepin   Jump rings

Materials

Six 25cm (10in) lengths of 3mm flat deer-hide leather lace

Six 7.5cm (3in) lengths 3mm flat deer-hide leather lace

One 35mm focal stone

One 7.5cm (3in) long 21-gauge eyepin

Two 19 x 5mm ribbon ends

One 20mm hook-and-eye clasp

Three 6mm jump rings

Toolkit

Ruler

Scissors

Round-nose pliers

Chain-nose pliers

Wire cutters

Tape

Glue

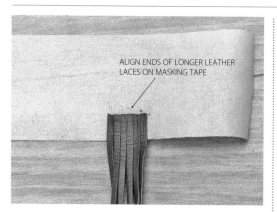

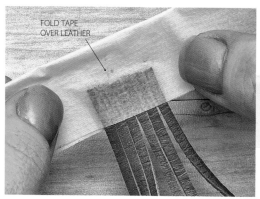

1 Prepare the leather for braiding by creating a binding of tape at one end. Lay out the ends of six 25cm (10in) lengths of leather side by side on a piece of tape.

ALIGN ENDS OF LONGER LEATHER LACES ON MASKING TAPE

2 Then, fold the edge of the tape over, sealing the ends inside. This creates a temporary casement to hold the leather strands in place as you work.

FOLD TAPE OVER LEATHER

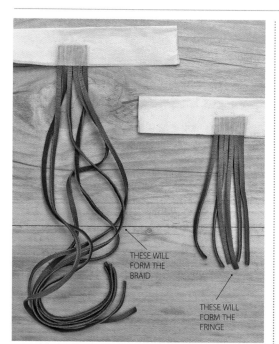

THESE WILL FORM THE BRAID

THESE WILL FORM THE FRINGE

3 Repeat this process for the six 7.5cm (3in) lengths of leather, which will become the fringe section.

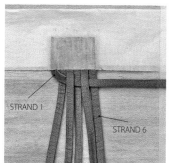

STRAND 1

STRAND 6

4 Tape the bound end of the 25cm (10in) leather laces to the worktop, ready to begin the six-strand braid. From left to right the strands of the braid are numbered 1 to 6. Take strand number 1, making sure that it remains flat and does not twist, and weave the strand towards the right by passing it over strand 2, under strand 3, over strand 4, under strand 5 and over strand 6.

5 Repeat this pattern for the next strand, always working from left to right. Strand 2 will now weave over 3, under 4, over 5, under 6 and over 1, which is now on the far right.

BRAID FOR 10.5CM (4¼IN)

6 Repeat this process for each strand until the braid is 10.5cm (4¼in) long.

APPLY GLUE
AT EACH END
OF BRAID

7 Once the braid has reached its finished length, tape down the loose strands. Apply a ribbon of glue at each end of the braid. Allow the glue to dry until it is tacky and holds its shape.

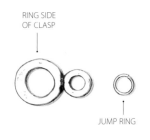

RING SIDE
OF CLASP

JUMP RING

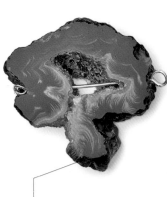

FOCAL STONE
WITH EYEPIN

APPLY GLUE
TO FRINGE

8 Apply a thin ribbon of glue just below the taped edge of the fringe section.

WIRE LOOP MADE USING ROUND-NOSE PLIERS

TRIM EXCESS WIRE

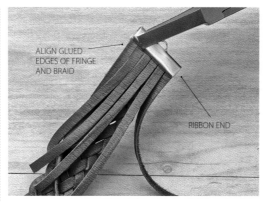

ALIGN GLUED EDGES OF FRINGE AND BRAID

RIBBON END

9 While the glue dries, put the focal stone on to an eyepin. Use round-nose pliers to form a simple wire loop, cutting off excess wire with wire cutters (see page 26).

10 Once the glue is dry, trim the taped ends of the braid and fringe sections, leaving thin slivers of tape. Use chain-nose pliers to crimp a ribbon end over one end of the braid. At the other end, lay the fringe section on top of the braid, line up the glued edges and crimp a ribbon end over both.

JUMP RING

JUMP RING

HOOK SIDE OF CLASP

USE CHAIN-NOSE PLIERS TO ATTACH JUMP RINGS AND CLASP

11 Now you are ready to assemble the cuff using jump rings. First, attach the hook part of the clasp to the fringe side of the braid. On the other side, attach the focal stone to the braid. Then, add the ring side of the clasp to the other side of the stone.

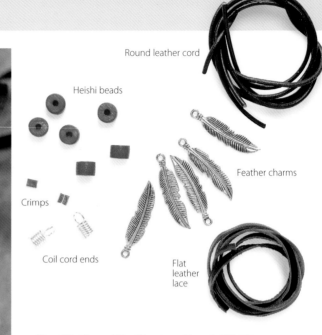

Round leather cord

Heishi beads

Crimps

Coil cord ends

Feather charms

Flat leather lace

RED FEATHER NECKLACE

Wear it long or wear it short – it is up to you with a tie-back necklace. Feather charms and bright beads are woven into a simple braid for a bohemian look in this project.

Materials

Three 30cm (12in) lengths of 1.5mm round leather cord

Two 40cm (16in) lengths of 3mm flat leather lace

Six 7 x 5mm heishi bone beads

Five 28 x 7mm feather charms

Two coil cord ends

Two 4 x 4mm square metal crimps

Toolkit

Ruler

Scissors

Chain-nose pliers

 Size

91cm (36in) long before tie

CRIMP COIL END ON TO ROUND CORDS

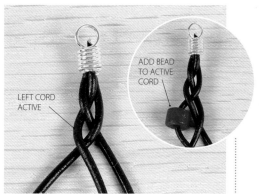

LEFT CORD ACTIVE

ADD BEAD TO ACTIVE CORD

3 HEISHI BONE BEADS

FEATHER CHARM

1 Crimp one coil cord end over the ends of the three round leather cords. Use chain-nose pliers to squeeze the last two coils of the cord end around the leather cords.

2 Begin a simple three-strand braid. After 2cm (¾in), when the next left cord becomes the active cord, string one heishi bone bead on to the left cord. Braid for another round and, when the next left cord becomes active, string on another heishi bead. Repeat this one more time, adding a third heishi bead before moving on.

3 Add one feather charm to the left cord when it becomes active again. Repeat for all five feather charms. As you braid, the cord will begin to curve with the addition of each bead or charm.

4 After all five of the feather charms are braided, add the final three heishi bone beads as before – one every time the left cord becomes active. Then, finish the braid with another 2cm (¾in) section of plain braid.

2CM (¾IN) PLAIN BRAID AFTER FINAL 3 HEISHI BEADS

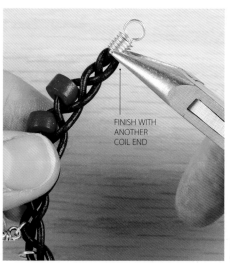

FINISH WITH ANOTHER COIL END

5 Trim the end of the braid and finish with a coil cord end as before.

FLAT LACE

CRIMP

6 Loop the end of a length of flat leather lace through one of the coil cord ends and secure with a metal crimp. Use chain-nose pliers to squeeze the crimp in place. Repeat at the other end of the braid.

Size

19cm (7½in) long

Ribbon ends

Wooden beads

Jump rings

Tube beads

Lobster clasp

Round leather cord

HARMONY CUFF

Learn how to create a basic interlocking pattern by weaving leather cord through a series of wooden and metal beads to make a simple yet sophisticated cuff bracelet.

Materials

Three 30cm (12in) lengths of 1mm round leather cord

Thirteen 10mm round wooden beads

Six 5 x 6mm metal tube beads

Two 10 x 5mm ribbon ends

One 15 x 13mm lobster clasp

Two 6mm jump rings

Toolkit

Ruler

Scissors

Chain-nose pliers

Tape

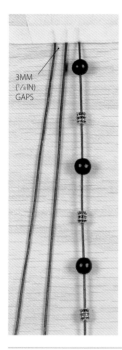

3MM
(¹/₈IN)
GAPS

1 Use tape to bind the ends of the three round leather cords with 3mm (¹/₈in) of space between them, then tape this to the worktop. On the right leather cord string a pattern of: 1 wooden bead, 1 metal tube, 1 wooden bead, 1 metal tube, 1 wooden bead, 1 metal tube.

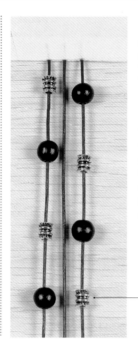

ALTERNATING PATTERN OF BEADS ON LEFT AND RIGHT CORDS

2 On the left leather cord string a pattern of: 1 metal tube, 1 wooden bead, 1 metal tube, 1 wooden bead, 1 metal tube, 1 wooden bead. Tape the ends of these two strands down to the worktop. Spread the beads out on the left and right cords so that they are evenly spaced.

WEAVE CENTRE CORD THROUGH METAL TUBE ON LEFT

3 String a wooden bead on to the centre cord, then weave the centre cord through the metal tube on the left. Space the beads evenly so that the right and left strands remain straight but the centre cord weaves from side to side.

WEAVE CENTRE CORD FROM SIDE TO SIDE

4 Slide another wooden bead on to the centre cord before weaving it through the next metal tube on the right. Continue this weaving pattern of adding a wooden bead before weaving through the next metal tube until the end. As you weave, keep the left and right cords straight. The finished woven section should measure 15cm (6in) from first to last bead. Adjust the beads on the cords so that they are evenly spaced and then remove the bracelet from the worktop.

6MM (¼IN) AT EACH END

RIBBON END

5 Trim the woven section so that there is 6mm (¼in) of space from the end beads. Crimp a ribbon end over each end of the woven bracelet using chain-nose pliers, taking care to keep the cords spaced evenly.

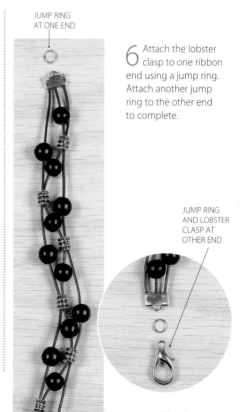

JUMP RING AT ONE END

JUMP RING AND LOBSTER CLASP AT OTHER END

6 Attach the lobster clasp to one ribbon end using a jump ring. Attach another jump ring to the other end to complete.

Gemstone beads

Round leather cord

Silk thread

Button

Materials

One 64cm (25in) length of 1mm round leather cord

Twenty-one 8mm round gemstone beads

One 1.8m (2yd) card of #3 silk thread with needle

One 15mm two-hole button

Toolkit

Ruler

Scissors

Tape

Glue

EAGLE BRACELET

This colourful gemstone bracelet is perfect for both men and women. This project introduces a style of loom weaving using gemstone beads, framed by leather cord and woven with silk thread in a contrasting colour.

Size
19cm (7½in) long

KNOT BUTTON ON TO MIDDLE OF CORD

1 String the round leather cord through the two holes of the metal button so that the button is in the middle of the cord. Tie an overhand knot with both ends of the cord just below the button to secure it in place.

ATTACH SILK THREAD TO LEFT CORD

2 Tie the end of the silk thread around the left strand of the leather cord, close to the button knot, and apply glue to the knot before trimming away the excess.

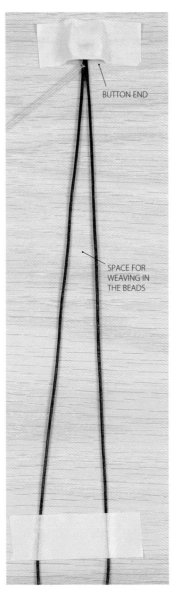

BUTTON END

SPACE FOR WEAVING IN THE BEADS

3 Tape the button and the ends of the leather cord to the worktop with a space between the cords to accommodate the width of the gemstone beads.

TAKE SILK THROUGH BEAD AND UNDER RIGHT CORD

TAKE SILK OVER RIGHT CORD, THROUGH BEAD AND UNDER LEFT CORD

4 String a gemstone bead on to the silk and pass the silk under the right leather cord. Coming around the right leather cord, thread the silk back through the bead in the opposite direction and then pass it under the left leather cord. Pull the silk snug so that the bead is nestled between the two cords. Take the silk around the left cord, add another gemstone bead and repeat the weaving motion for the new bead. Repeat for all 21 beads.

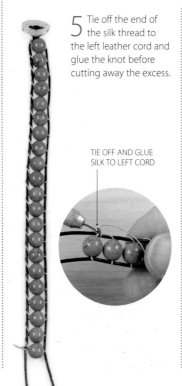

5 Tie off the end of the silk thread to the left leather cord and glue the knot before cutting away the excess.

TIE OFF AND GLUE SILK TO LEFT CORD

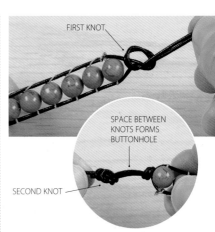

FIRST KNOT

SPACE BETWEEN KNOTS FORMS BUTTONHOLE

SECOND KNOT

6 Remove the bracelet from the worktop and tie an overhand knot with both leather cords against the last bead. Make a second overhand knot 13mm (½in) away from the first to create a buttonhole. Trim excess leather cord to 6mm (¼in).

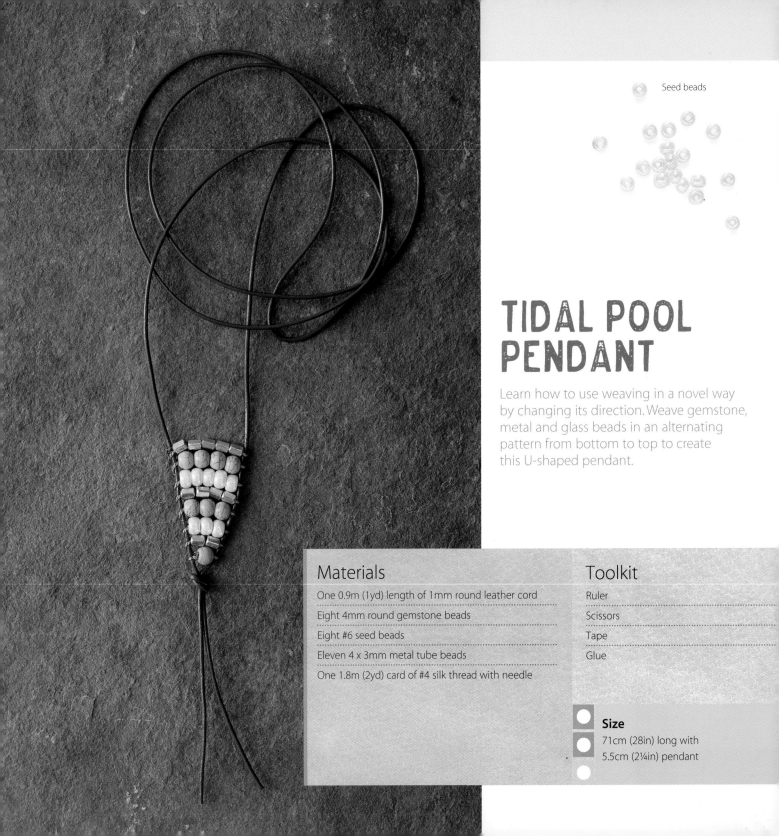

Seed beads

TIDAL POOL PENDANT

Learn how to use weaving in a novel way by changing its direction. Weave gemstone, metal and glass beads in an alternating pattern from bottom to top to create this U-shaped pendant.

Materials

One 0.9m (1yd) length of 1mm round leather cord

Eight 4mm round gemstone beads

Eight #6 seed beads

Eleven 4 x 3mm metal tube beads

One 1.8m (2yd) card of #4 silk thread with needle

Toolkit

Ruler

Scissors

Tape

Glue

Size

71cm (28in) long with 5.5cm (2¼in) pendant

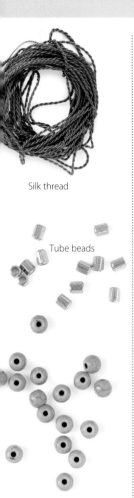

Silk thread

Tube beads

Gemstone beads

Round
leather cord

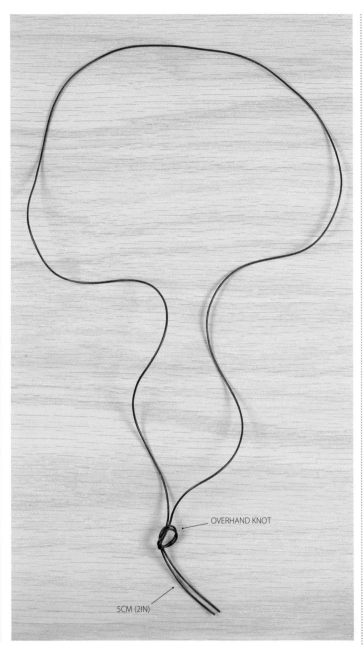

OVERHAND KNOT

5CM (2IN)

1 Fold the length of round leather cord in half and tie an
overhand knot 5cm (2in) from the end. This forms the
basic layout of the finished necklace.

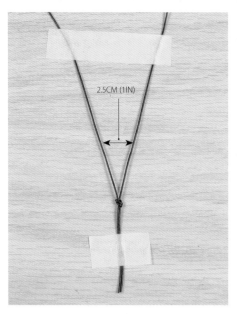

2.5CM (1IN)

2 Tape the leather to the worktop with the knot at
the bottom and a 2.5cm (1in) space between the
leather cords approximately where the top of
the pendant will be.

ATTACH SILK
TO LEFT CORD

PINPOIN
WATCH

3 Tie the end of the silk thread around the left
leather cord just above the knot and apply glue
to the knot before trimming away the excess.

WEAVE SILK AROUND
CORDS AND THROUGH
GEMSTONE BEAD

WEAVE SILK AROUND
CORDS AND THROUGH
TUBE BEADS

WEAVE SILK AROUND
CORDS AND THROUGH
SEED BEADS

3CM
(1¼IN)
HIGH

4 String a gemstone bead on to the silk and pass the silk under the right leather cord. Coming around the right leather cord, thread the silk back through the bead in the opposite direction and pass the silk under the left leather cord. Pull the silk snug so that the bead is nestled between the two leather cords. Bring the silk around the left cord and through two tube beads, repeating the weaving motion for the new row. Next, add a row of seed beads the width needed to fit between the leather cords and weave as before. Make sure that the number of beads increases to fit the widening space between the leather cords. Repeat this process, alternating rows of gemstone beads, tube beads and seed beads, until the woven section measures 3cm (1¼in) high.

Adjust the number of beads in each row to create the triangular shape.

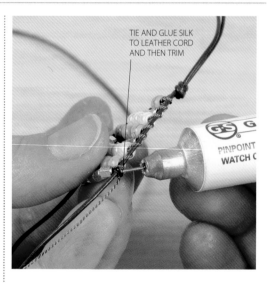

TIE AND GLUE SILK
TO LEATHER CORD
AND THEN TRIM

5 Tie the end of the silk thread to the right leather cord. Remove the necklace from the worktop and glue the knot before cutting away the excess.

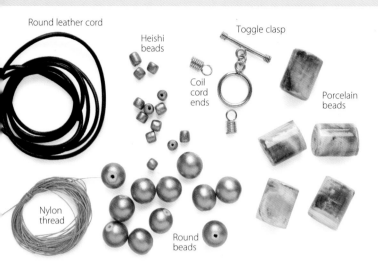

Round leather cord

Heishi beads

Coil cord ends

Toggle clasp

Porcelain beads

Nylon thread

Round beads

DESERT QUEEN NECKLACE

This woven necklace cries glamour and style. Use large statement beads in this weaving pattern to create a dramatic bib necklace.

Materials

One 43cm (17in) length of 1.5mm round leather cord

One 51cm (20in) length of 1.5mm round leather cord

Five 22 x 16mm porcelain tube beads

Ten 12mm round metallic wood beads

Fourteen 4 x 3mm heishi metallic wood beads

One 3.2m (3½yd) length of #3 or 0.5mm nylon thread

Two coil cord ends

One 15mm toggle clasp

Toolkit

Ruler

Scissors

Chain-nose pliers

Thread burner

Two beading needles

Tape

 Size
51cm (20in) long

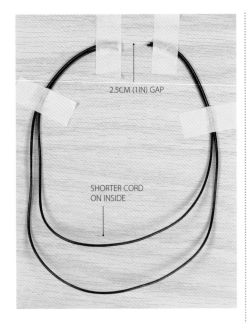

2.5CM (1IN) GAP

SHORTER CORD
ON INSIDE

1 Line up the ends of the round leather cords to form an oval, with the ends about 2.5cm (1in) apart. Tape down the ends and the sides to the worktop, with the longer cord on the bottom. This forms the basic outline of the necklace.

WEAVE THREAD THROUGH
BEAD, AROUND TOP CORD
AND THROUGH BEAD AGAIN

2 Find the centre of the nylon thread and tape it down to the worktop just below the bottom centre of the leather cords. Thread a beading needle on to each end of the nylon. Slide the first porcelain bead on to the uppermost end of the nylon thread and place the bead between the two leather cords. Weave the thread under the top cord and then around the cord and back through the bead in the opposite direction.

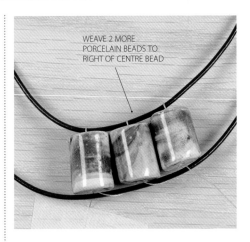

WEAVE 2 MORE
PORCELAIN BEADS TO
RIGHT OF CENTRE BEAD

3 Take the thread around the bottom cord and repeat this process with two more porcelain beads to the right of the first. Make sure they follow the shape of the necklace. The tops should touch and the bottoms should be spaced slightly apart.

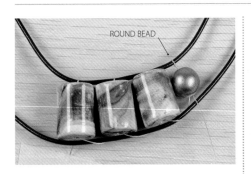

ROUND BEAD

4 Slide the first round bead on to the thread and continue weaving as before. The round beads are smaller than the porcelain beads, so the space between the cords will need to be smaller as well. Make sure as you pull the thread tight that you keep the bead spaced evenly between the cords. This will maintain a nice curve in the necklace shape. Repeat this process with four more round beads.

HEISHI BEAD

5 Now string on the first heishi bead and weave it between the cords as before, keeping it evenly spaced between them. Repeat with six more heishi beads. When seven heishi beads have been woven, take a moment to make sure the curve of the necklace is consistent and gently pull on the leather cords to reposition any beads that are out of place. When this is done, pull the nylon thread tight and tape it down to the worktop.

WEAVE BEADS ON TO LEFT SIDE OF NECKLACE TO MIRROR RIGHT SIDE

6 Untape the other end of the nylon cord from the worktop to begin weaving the other half of the necklace. Weaving on this side will be the opposite of the first half. Pass over then under the bottom cord before adding a porcelain bead. Pass over and around the top cord before weaving back through the bead and over the bottom cord. Repeat this step, mirroring the pattern from the other side with two porcelain beads, five round beads and seven heishi beads. When finished, check the curve of the necklace and tape down the nylon thread as before.

WEAVE THREAD AROUND CORDS IN A FIGURE-OF-EIGHT

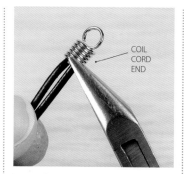

13MM (½IN) LONG

7 Remove the right nylon thread from the worktop and, after the last bead, begin weaving a figure-of-eight around the two leather cords. This figure-of-eight will follow the same weaving pattern as the rest of the right side, only without a bead at the centre. The thread will pass over the bottom cord, under and around the top cord, and back under and around the bottom cord. Repeat until the section is 13mm (½in) long.

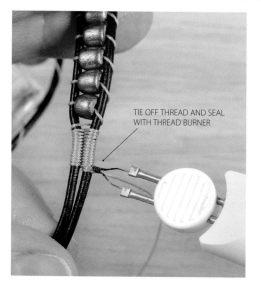

TIE OFF THREAD AND SEAL WITH THREAD BURNER

8 Tie off the end of the nylon cord and seal the knot with a thread burner before trimming away the excess. Repeat steps 7–8 on the left side of the necklace.

COIL CORD END

9 Remove the necklace from the worktop and crimp a coil cord end over each end, using chain-nose pliers to squeeze the last two coils of the cord end to hold it securely in place.

TOGGLE CLASP

10 Attach a toggle clasp to the coil cord ends to complete.

MACRAMÉ

Cords may seem to know how to knot themselves all on their own, but it takes some skill to make a beautiful knot. Macramé is a versatile technique that can be done with almost any fibre, but with leather it takes on a distinct look. Leather, because of its body, creates looser, more dynamic knots that really stand out. Adding beads makes them even more impressive. The following projects demonstrate different ways of using all kinds of knots, from the most basic half-hitch knot to the elaborate Josephine knot.

Materials

Four 38cm (15in) lengths of
1mm round leather cord

Two colours of #6 seed beads

Two coil cord ends

One 10 x 6mm lobster clasp

One 6mm jump ring

Toolkit

Ruler

Scissors

Chain-nose pliers

Tape

Size
19cm (7½in) long

CELTIC KNOT FRIENDSHIP BRACELET

Here is a project for you and your best friend. The Celtic knot resembles an infinity symbol to show that your friendship is forever, so why not make a matching set.

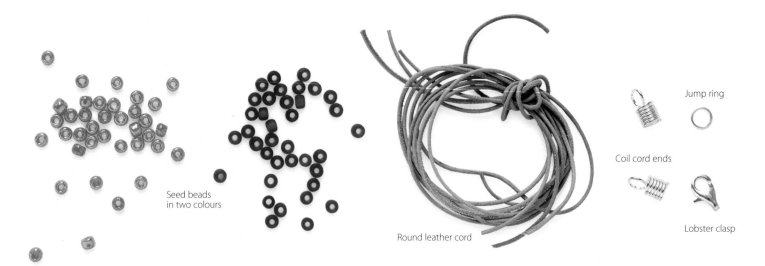

Seed beads
in two colours

Round leather cord

Jump ring

Coil cord ends

Lobster clasp

LOOP RIGHT END
OVER THE LEFT

1 Line up two pieces of round leather cord, folded in half to form a loop. With the loop facing you, overlap the right tail end over the left. Tape down the ends of the cords.

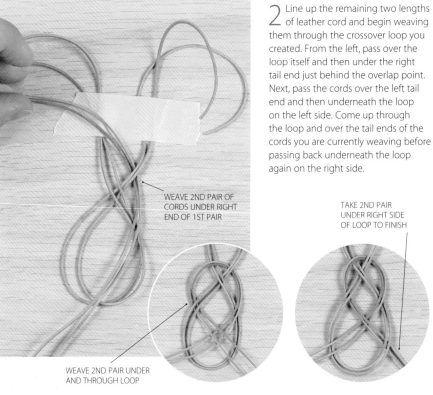

WEAVE 2ND PAIR OF
CORDS UNDER RIGHT
END OF 1ST PAIR

WEAVE 2ND PAIR UNDER
AND THROUGH LOOP

TAKE 2ND PAIR
UNDER RIGHT SIDE
OF LOOP TO FINISH

2 Line up the remaining two lengths of leather cord and begin weaving them through the crossover loop you created. From the left, pass over the loop itself and then under the right tail end just behind the overlap point. Next, pass the cords over the left tail end and then underneath the loop on the left side. Come up through the loop and over the tail ends of the cords you are currently weaving before passing back underneath the loop again on the right side.

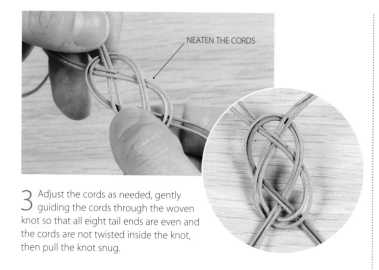

NEATEN THE CORDS

3 Adjust the cords as needed, gently guiding the cords through the woven knot so that all eight tail ends are even and the cords are not twisted inside the knot, then pull the knot snug.

STRING OTHER COLOUR BEADS ON TO FOUR INNER TAIL ENDS

5 String 7cm (2¾in) of the second colour of seed beads on to the four inner tail end cords.

6 Trim the ends of the cords to 6mm (¼in) away from the beads and use chain-nose pliers to crimp a coil cord end over all four cords on each side of the knot. Take care not to crush the beads. Attach a lobster clasp to one cord end and a jump ring to the other to finish.

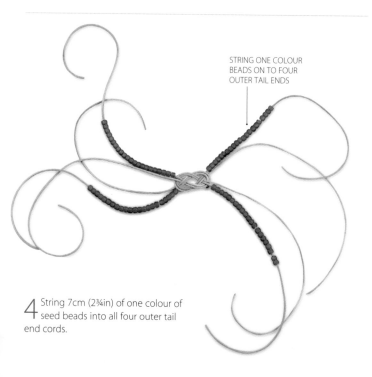

STRING ONE COLOUR BEADS ON TO FOUR OUTER TAIL ENDS

4 String 7cm (2¾in) of one colour of seed beads into all four outer tail end cords.

COIL CORD END

LOBSTER CLASP

LOTUS BRACELET

If you crochet, you will already be familiar with a chain stitch. A chain stitch in leather, however, is a unique look indeed. No crochet hook required.

Materials

One 1.5m (5ft) length of 0.5mm round leather cord

Nine 4mm round glass beads

One 16.5mm two-hole button

Two 4 x 4mm square metal crimps

Toolkit

Ruler

Scissors

Chain-nose pliers

Tape

Size

19cm (7½in) long

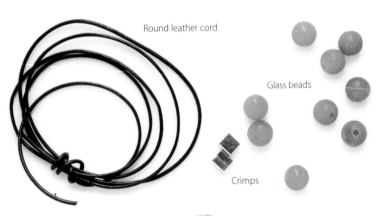

Round leather cord

Glass beads

Crimps

Button

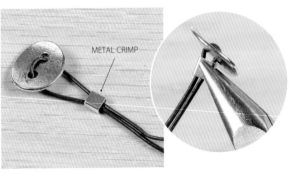

METAL CRIMP

1 Thread one end of the round leather cord through the holes of the button. Slide a crimp over both cord ends and squeeze with chain-nose pliers to secure the button in place. Do a tug test to make sure it is secure, then trim away the excess cord.

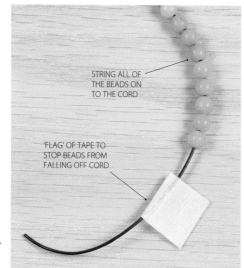

STRING ALL OF
THE BEADS ON
TO THE CORD

'FLAG' OF TAPE TO
STOP BEADS FROM
FALLING OFF CORD

2 String all of the
beads on to the
cord and add a piece
of tape at the end like
a flag to prevent them
from falling off. For now,
leave these beads at
the end of the cord.

PULL A LOOP
THROUGH KNOT

3 To make the first chain
stitch, begin to make an
overhand knot, but only pull
a small loop of cord through
instead of the whole tail end, then
pull the knot tight. For the next
chain, pull a loop of the cord
through the first loop, then pull
the first loop tight. Repeat until
there is 13mm (½in) of chain
stitches extending from the
button. As the chains build next
to each other, they will begin to
form what looks like a chain link.

KEEP PULLING LOOPS
THROUGH TO FORM
CHAIN STITCHES

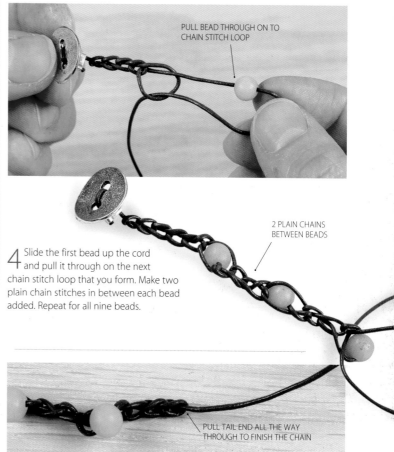

PULL BEAD THROUGH ON TO
CHAIN STITCH LOOP

2 PLAIN CHAINS
BETWEEN BEADS

4 Slide the first bead up the cord
and pull it through on the next
chain stitch loop that you form. Make two
plain chain stitches in between each bead
added. Repeat for all nine beads.

PULL TAIL END ALL THE WAY
THROUGH TO FINISH THE CHAIN

5 Make 13mm (½in) more of plain chain stitches before finally
pulling the tail of the leather cord through the last loop to finish.

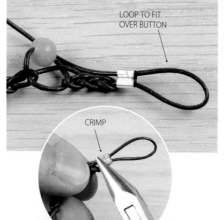

LOOP TO FIT
OVER BUTTON

CRIMP

6 Add a crimp to the
end of the chain of
stitches. Make a 1.5cm
(⅝in) loop with the cord
by threading it back
through the crimp to
form a button loop. Crimp
using chain-nose pliers
to secure, and trim
away excess.

Silk thread

Round beads

Spike beads

Hoop earrings

Flat suede lace

STARGAZER EARRINGS

Add a pop of colour and glamour to an otherwise plain pair of hoop earrings, using colourful suede lace to form square knots, with beads between the knots.

Materials

Two 127cm (50in) lengths of 3mm flat suede lace

Eight 4mm round metal beads

Eight 13 x 5mm top-drilled spike beads

One 1.8m (2yd) card of #6 silk thread with needle

Two 50mm (2in) diameter hoop earrings

Toolkit

Ruler

Scissors

Glue

Size
50mm (2in)
diameter

KNOT MIDDLE OF LACE ON TO FRONT OF HOOP

1 Take one length of flat suede lace and fold it in half to find the centre. Place the front of one of the hoop earrings into the loop and tie a knot around the hoop.

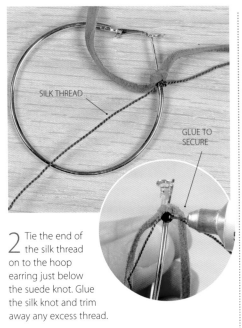

SILK THREAD

GLUE TO
SECURE

2 Tie the end of
the silk thread
on to the hoop
earring just below
the suede knot. Glue
the silk knot and trim
away any excess thread.

TAKE RIGHT LACE ACROSS
FRONT OF HOOP

THREAD LEFT LACE THROUGH
HOOP AND LOOP CREATED
BY RIGHT LACE

3 With the edge of the hoop in front of you, form the first square
knot by placing the right end of the suede lace across the front
of the hoop, leaving a loop on the right side of the hoop. Next,
place the left suede lace over the top of the right lace, pass it
through the hoop and up through the loop formed by the right
lace, and pull tight. Now reverse the process, taking the left lace
across the hoop earring, placing the right lace over the tail end of
the left, then passing it through the hoop and back up through the
loop formed by the lace on the opposite side. Repeat this process
four more times over both the hoop and the silk.

4 Slide a round metal bead on to the
silk thread, up to the last square
knot with the bead on the outside of
the hoop. Hold the bead in place and
make two more square knots just
below it. Repeat this with a second
round bead.

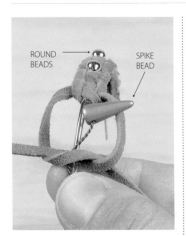

ROUND
BEADS

SPIKE
BEAD

5 Slide a spike bead on to the silk
thread up to the last knot and
make two more square knots just
below it on the hoop. Repeat with
three more spike beads.

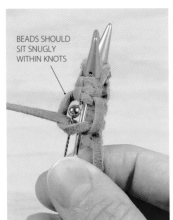

BEADS SHOULD
SIT SNUGLY
WITHIN KNOTS

6 Repeat this process with two more
round metal beads.

SECURE AND
TRIM THE
SILK THREAD

7 After the last bead, make four
more square knots over both the
hoop and the silk. Tie off the silk
thread, securing the knot with glue
and trimming away the excess.

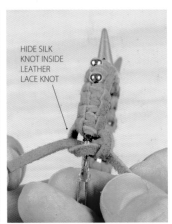

HIDE SILK
KNOT INSIDE
LEATHER
LACE KNOT

8 Make one more square knot with
the suede lace to hide the silk
knot. Run a thin ribbon of glue along
the last knot on the inside of the hoop
earring to secure, and trim away the
extra suede when the glue is dry.
Repeat all steps for the second earring.

Seed beads

Hook earwires

Round leather cord

NAUTICAL KNOT EARRINGS

The art of knotting is well known to any sailor. For this project, learn how to add beads to a complicated knot to create nautical-inspired earrings.

Materials

Two 51cm (20in) lengths of 0.5mm round leather cord

#6 seed beads

Two hook earwires

Toolkit

Ruler

Scissors

Chain-nose pliers

Size
9cm (3½in) long

LOOP 12.5CM (5IN) FROM ONE END

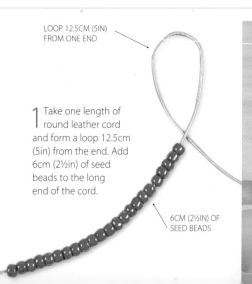

1 Take one length of round leather cord and form a loop 12.5cm (5in) from the end. Add 6cm (2½in) of seed beads to the long end of the cord.

6CM (2½IN) OF SEED BEADS

13MM (½IN) GAP BETWEEN LOOP AND BEADS

TAKE TAIL END OF CORD AROUND BASE OF ORIGINAL LOOP AND OVER TO LEFT

2 Form a loop with the beaded section, pointing in the opposite direction from the original loop. Cross the end of the cord over the front of original loop 13mm (½in) from the beads, then take the cord under the original loop from left to right and around the front again to the left side.

1ST LOOP OF BEADS
2ND LOOP OF BEADS

3 Add 5cm (2in) of seed beads to the end of the cord and make another loop just inside the first beaded loop.

1ST CROSSOVER
2ND CROSSOVER

4 Cross the end of the cord over the original loop so that the cord lies immediately below the first crossover. Pass the cord underneath and around the front to the left side as before.

3RD LOOP OF BEADS

5 Add 4cm (1½in) of seed beads and form one last loop inside the others.

3RD CROSSOVER

6 Cross the end of the cord over just below the second crossover. Pass the end of the cord under the loop and back up over the other side.

THREAD TAIL END THROUGH TO BACK

KNOT TAIL ENDS AT BACK BELOW CROSSOVERS

7 Pull the tail end of the cord through the centre beaded loop. Flip the earring over and tie an overhand knot with both tail ends just below the last crossover.

KNOT 3 BEADS ON TO EACH TAIL

8 Add three seed beads to each tail end and tie a final knot to secure 5cm (2in) down from the knot just below the crossovers.

USE CHAIN-NOSE PLIERS TO ATTACH EARWIRE TO TOP LOOP

9 Attach an earwire to the original top loop to finish. Repeat all steps for the second earring.

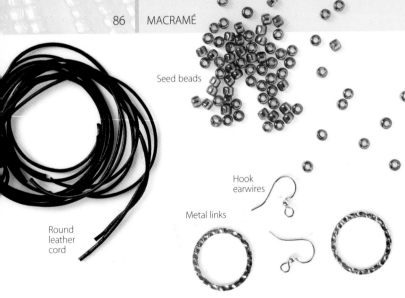

Seed beads

Hook earwires

Metal links

Round leather cord

CASABLANCA EARRINGS

Macramé knots can be used in a variety of ways, depending on the desired look. The double half-hitch knot creates an interesting texture that looks like woven fabric, creating a beautiful chevron pattern in these earrings. Finish them off with a beaded fringe for a flirty bohemian look.

Materials

Six 36cm (14in) lengths of 1mm round leather cord

#6 glass seed beads

Two 20mm round metal links

Two hook earwires

Toolkit

Ruler

Scissors

Chain-nose pliers

Size
8cm (3¼in) long

1 Use lark's head knots to attach three lengths of round leather cord to a metal link (see page 21). Make sure that all of the knots are facing the same direction.

2 Tape the metal link down on to the worktop. The cords are numbered 1–6 from left to right. Lay cord 1 across the others at a 45-degree angle and tape it down. To make a double half-hitch knot, take cord 2 from under cord 1 and pass it over and around cord 1, leaving a loop on the left side. Bring cord 2 through the loop and pull the knot tight (above left). Repeat for the second half of the double knot. Then make a double half-hitch knot with cord 3 over cord 1 and pull tight (above right).

3 Repeat this pattern going the other way, starting by laying cord 6 across the others at a 45-degree angle and taping it down. Make a double half-hitch knot with cord 5 over cord 6 (above), and then with cord 4 over cord 6. The right side will be a mirror image of the left side.

4 When done, untape cords 1 and 6 from the worktop and knot them together.

5 Repeat steps 2–4 twice more for a total of three rows of double half-hitch knots. For the final knot at the centre, make a square knot to secure (see page 23).

6 Remove the project from the table and pull the cords gently to make them hang straighter. Add 4cm (1½in) of seed beads to each cord and make an overhand knot to secure. Trim each cord to 6mm (¼in) from the final knot.

7 Use chain-nose pliers to add an earwire to the top of the metal link to complete the earring. Repeat to make a second earring.

AZTEC GEMSTONE NECKLACE

The half-hitch knot is a simple macramé knot that creates a helix shape, which gives this necklace its unique look, with the soft leather cord spiralling around an asymmetrical pattern of gemstone beads. A silk-covered button loop made using lark's head sennit knots and a button clasp finish the design with a bright pop of colour.

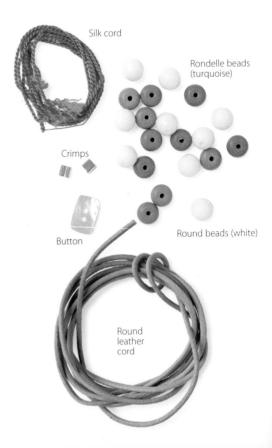

Silk cord

Rondelle beads (turquoise)

Crimps

Button

Round beads (white)

Round leather cord

Size

53cm (21in) long

Materials

One 2.3m (2.5yd) length of 1.5mm round leather cord

Fifty 8 x 6mm rondelle beads

Eighteen 8mm round beads

One 1.8m (2yd) card of #14 silk cord in contrasting colour with needle

One 13mm (½in) two-hole button

Two 4 x 4mm square metal crimps

Toolkit

Ruler

Scissors

Chain-nose pliers

Tape

TWO-HOLE BUTTON

KNOT SILK CORD AROUND LEATHER BEHIND BUTTON

4CM (1½IN) LEATHER TAIL

1 Thread the leather cord through the holes of the button. Most of the cord should be on one side and about 4cm (1½in) on the other. Tie an overhand knot around the leather just behind the button with the tail end of the silk cord and pull tight.

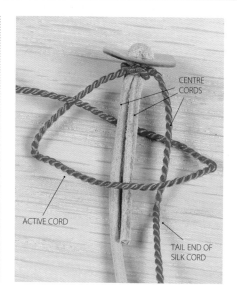

CENTRE CORDS

ACTIVE CORD

TAIL END OF SILK CORD

2 The two leather cords and the tail of the silk are now referred to as the 'centre cords', and the long silk cord as the 'active cord'. To make the first half-hitch knot, start with the active cord on the left side of the project. Lay the active cord over the three centre cords, leaving an opening between the centre cords and the active cord on the left. Thread the active cord around and under all three centre cords from the right and bring it up through the opening on the left. Pull the active cord tight to complete the knot.

THREE HALF-HITCH KNOTS

3 Repeat step 2 to make two more half-hitch knots with the silk cord.

CRIMP ALL CORDS TOGETHER

4 Slide a metal crimp over all four ends of the leather and silk cords. Use chain-nose pliers to squeeze the crimp closed. Cut the tail end of the silk and the tail end of the leather cord flush with the crimp.

5 String all of the beads on to the silk cord in the following order: 3 rondelle, 1 round, 2 rondelle, 1 round, 5 rondelle, 2 round. Repeat the pattern a total of five times, omitting the last two round beads on the last repetition.

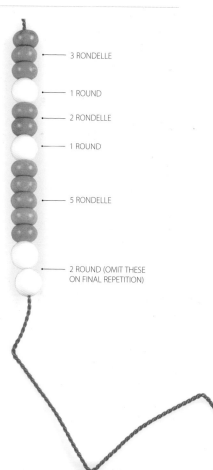

3 RONDELLE

1 ROUND

2 RONDELLE

1 ROUND

5 RONDELLE

2 ROUND (OMIT THESE ON FINAL REPETITION)

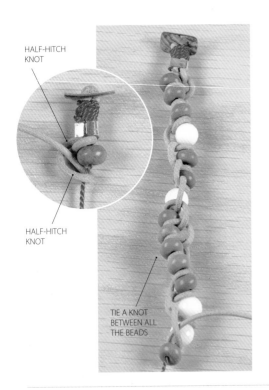

HALF-HITCH
KNOT

HALF-HITCH
KNOT

TIE A KNOT
BETWEEN ALL
THE BEADS

6 Tape the silk cord to the worktop with the button at the top, leaving space between the crimp and the beads to allow room to work. The leather cord is now the active cord, and the silk is the centre cord. Make a half-hitch knot with the leather cord and push it up to the crimp. This knot will be looser than those made with the silk. This is correct – do not pull the leather cord too tight; it should gently hug the silk cord. Push the first bead up to the knot and make another half-hitch knot below it. Repeat this process for all the beads. After a few knots, you will begin to see how the leather cord will make a helix around the beads. The cords will twist around themselves as you make the knots, so remove the tape and readjust the project as needed.

SLIDE CRIMP ON TO
BOTH CORDS BUT
DON'T TIGHTEN

7 After the last half-hitch knot, add a second crimp over both the leather and silk cords but do not squeeze closed yet.

8 The button-loop end of the clasp is formed by using the silk cord to make a row of lark's head sennit knots over the leather cord. The silk cord is the active cord, and the leather cord is the centre cord. Start with the active cord on the left side of the project. Lay the active cord over the centre cord, leaving a space on the left between the two cords. Thread the active cord underneath the centre cord and up through the space, pulling it tight. This is the same as a half-hitch knot. The second half of a lark's head sennit knot is a mirror image of the first half. Start with the active cord on the right side of the project and lay it over the centre cord, leaving a space on the right. Thread the end of the active cord under the centre cord and up through the space. Pull the knot tight. Continue making a row of knots for about 4cm (1½in); there should be about 14 knots.

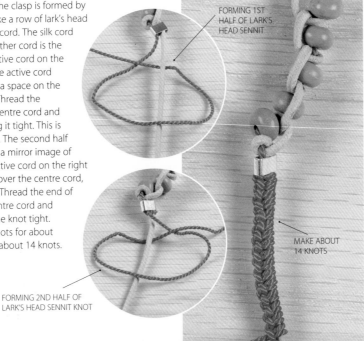

FORMING 1ST
HALF OF LARK'S
HEAD SENNIT

MAKE ABOUT
14 KNOTS

FORMING 2ND HALF OF
LARK'S HEAD SENNIT KNOT

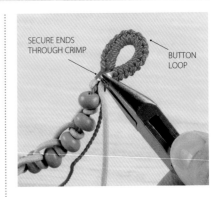

SECURE ENDS
THROUGH CRIMP

BUTTON
LOOP

9 Fold the silk-covered leather cord in half, creating a 13mm (½in) button loop. Thread both the silk and leather cords back through the crimp and squeeze it in place with chain-nose pliers. Trim the ends of the silk and leather flush with the crimp.

Size

18cm (7in) long

Materials

One 46cm (18in) length of 1.5mm round leather cord

Eleven 12mm large-hole round pearl beads

One 1.8m (2yd) card of #14 or 1mm nylon cord with needle

One 16.5mm shank button

One 6mm jump ring

Toolkit

Ruler

Scissors

Thread burner

SOUTH SEA PEARL CUFF

Sometimes all you need is a pop of colour to take your jewellery designs to the next level. This project weaves a contrasting coloured thread between two leather cords, with the thread knotted to the leather with lark's head sennit knots between large faux pearls.

Pearl beads

Button

Jump ring

Nylon cord

Round leather cord

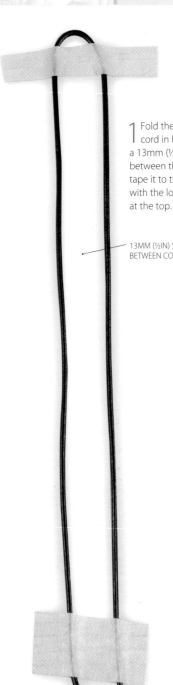

1 Fold the round leather cord in half, leaving a 13mm (½in) space between the cords, and tape it to the worktop with the looped end at the top.

13MM (½IN) SPACE BETWEEN CORDS

ATTACH NYLON CORD 1.5CM (⅝IN) BELOW TOP OF LEATHER LOOP

2 Tie one end of the nylon cord to the left leather cord, 1.5cm (⅝in) away from the end of the loop, and seal the knot with a thread burner.

FORMING 1ST HALF OF LARK'S HEAD SENNIT KNOT

FORMING 2ND HALF OF LARK'S HEAD SENNIT

3 Tie the nylon cord around the right leather cord with a lark's head sennit knot. To form the first half of the knot, lay the nylon cord over the right leather cord, then thread it under the leather and pull the tail end through just above where the nylon cord first passed over the leather. To form the second half of the knot, pass the end of the nylon under the leather from the left, leaving a loop of nylon cord on the left side of the right leather cord. Coming around the leather cord from right to left, pass the nylon over the leather and down through the nylon loop on the other side. Pull tight to secure, making sure that the space between the leather cords remains consistent.

1ST KNOT

2ND KNOT

4 Make another lark's head sennit knot over the left leather cord. This knot should be a mirror image of the knot just made on the right cord.

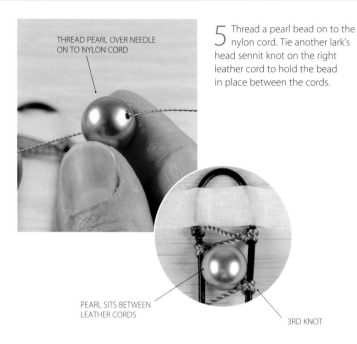

THREAD PEARL OVER NEEDLE ON TO NYLON CORD

5 Thread a pearl bead on to the nylon cord. Tie another lark's head sennit knot on the right leather cord to hold the bead in place between the cords.

PEARL SITS BETWEEN LEATHER CORDS

3RD KNOT

4TH KNOT

6 Make another lark's head sennit knot over the left leather cord. Repeat steps 5–6 to add all of the pearls, then remove the project from the worktop.

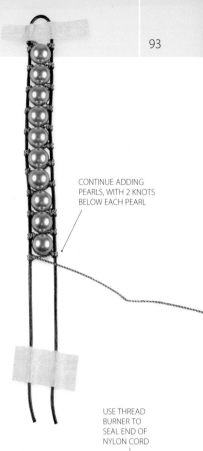

CONTINUE ADDING PEARLS, WITH 2 KNOTS BELOW EACH PEARL

USE THREAD BURNER TO SEAL END OF NYLON CORD

13MM (½IN) BETWEEN BUTTON AND KNOT

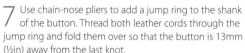

ATTACH JUMP RING TO BUTTON SHANK

7 Use chain-nose pliers to add a jump ring to the shank of the button. Thread both leather cords through the jump ring and fold them over so that the button is 13mm (½in) away from the last knot.

TIE 3 KNOTS UP TO BUTTON SHANK

8 Using the nylon cord, tie three lark's head sennit knots around all four leather cords up to the jump ring. Make these knots as tight as possible to hold the leather cords securely in place.

9 Use a thread burner to seal the last knot in place and then trim the leather cord flush.

FREE SPIRIT PENDANT

Do you have a special stone or crystal that you absolutely love but don't know how to use because it does not have a hole? This project shows you how to turn it into a necklace by creating a basket with macramé knots to hold your precious gem.

Seed beads

Flat suede lace

Focal stone

Materials

Three 2.1m (7ft) lengths of 2mm flat suede lace

One 30–40mm undrilled focal stone

Eighteen #6 glass seed beads

Toolkit

Ruler

Scissors

Size

76cm (30in) long with 12.5cm (5in) pendant

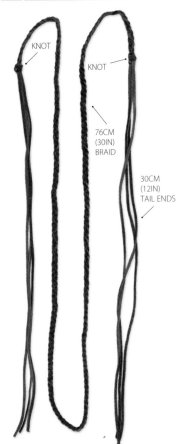

KNOT

KNOT

76CM (30IN) BRAID

30CM (12IN) TAIL ENDS

1 Make an overhand knot with all three suede laces 30cm (12in) from the end. Braid a simple three-strand braid that is 76cm (30in) long and tie off the end with another overhand knot. For a cleaner look, make sure that the laces remain flat as you braid. Trim the second side of the braid so that both loose sides are 30cm (12in) long.

ORIGINAL 2 KNOTS

KNOT ALL 6 LACES TOGETHER

2 Fold over the braid so that the knots align, then tie the ends of all six laces together with another overhand knot.

SEPARATE THE 6 LACES

3 Separate out the six laces and make a row of three square knots using pairs of adjacent laces (see page 23). Keep these knots close to the large overhand knot.

TIE ADJACENT PAIRS OF LACES WITH SQUARE KNOTS

2ND ROW OF SQUARE KNOTS

4 Make another row of square knots, this time knotting laces from two neighbouring knots together to form a mesh. Space this second set of knots about 6mm (¼in) below the first row.

TIE STONE WITHIN MESH OF SQUARE KNOTS

5 Place the focal stone inside the mesh of square knots and start knotting the suede laces around it, alternating the pairs of laces to form a mesh basket. Continue to make rows of square knots, fitting the basket to the stone so that the stone is held snugly inside.

OVERHAND KNOT

6 When you reach the bottom of the stone and the last row of square knots is very close together, form an overhand knot just beneath the stone.

5CM (2IN) BEADED TASSEL

7 Add three seed beads to each lace and tie an overhand knot 5cm (2in) from the bottom of the pendant. Trim the excess to 6mm (¼in) to finish.

GYPSY CUFF

This striking bangle utilises a focal link that grabs attention but does not outshine the three beaded leather strands that make up most of the bracelet. The thick leather cords are wrapped with embroidery thread using chain stitch.

Gemstone beads

Crimps

Focal link

Size

20cm (8in) circumference

Materials

Three 30cm (12in) lengths of 1.5mm round leather cord

Two skeins of silk or cotton embroidery thread in complementary colours

One 40cm (16in) strand of 4mm round gemstone beads

One 42 x 22mm metal focal link

Two 11 x 4mm rectangular metal crimps

Toolkit

Ruler

Scissors

Chain-nose pliers

Beading needle

Tape

Glue

Embroidery thread in two colours

Round leather cord

TIE THREAD 6CM (2½IN) FROM END OF LEATHER CORD

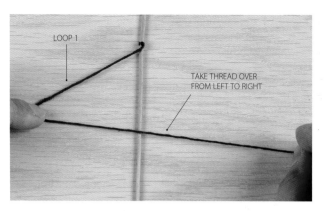

LOOP 1

TAKE THREAD OVER FROM LEFT TO RIGHT

1 Pull out about a metre of embroidery thread from the skein to work with, but keep most of it wrapped together for ease of use. Thread a beading needle on to the end of the skein and string 18 gemstone beads on to the thread. Remove the needle. Tape one length of round leather cord down on to the worktop at top and bottom, then use a double overhand knot to tie the tail end of the embroidery thread to the leather cord about 6cm (2½in) from the end of the leather. Glue the knot and trim away excess embroidery thread when dry. Lay the thread over the leather cord from left to right, leaving a loop on the left side between the thread and the cord.

2 Pass a small loop of thread under the leather from right to left, bringing it up through the original loop on the left. Pull the original loop tight to form the first chain stitch.

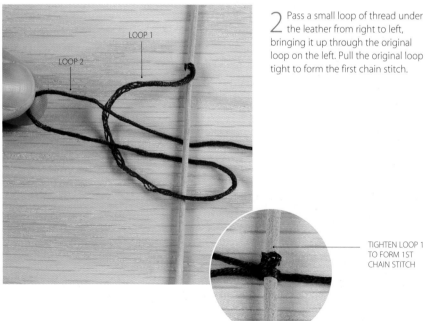

LOOP 1

LOOP 2

TIGHTEN LOOP 1 TO FORM 1ST CHAIN STITCH

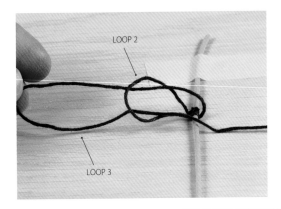

LOOP 2

LOOP 3

3 Wrap the thread over the leather cord, pull a small loop through the previous loop and pull it tight to form the second chain stitch. Repeat this step, alternating passing the loop under the leather cord and over it for 13mm (½in).

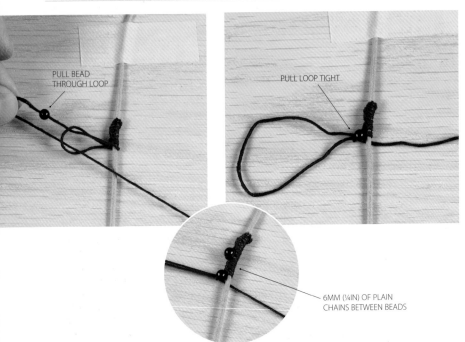

PULL BEAD THROUGH LOOP

PULL LOOP TIGHT

6MM (¼IN) OF PLAIN CHAINS BETWEEN BEADS

4 Slide a bead up the thread and through the previous loop, then pull the loop tight. Work 6mm (¼in) of plain chain stitches and then pull another bead through on the next loop. Pull another loop through to tighten the first beaded chain in place. Repeat this process for all of the beads, with 6mm (¼in) of plain chain stitches between beads.

5 Once all of the beads have been added, work another 13mm (½in) of plain chain stitches. Cut the rest of the skein off and pull the last piece of thread all the way through to finish the last chain. Glue the last chain and trim away the excess.

13MM (½IN) OF PLAIN CHAINS AFTER LAST BEAD

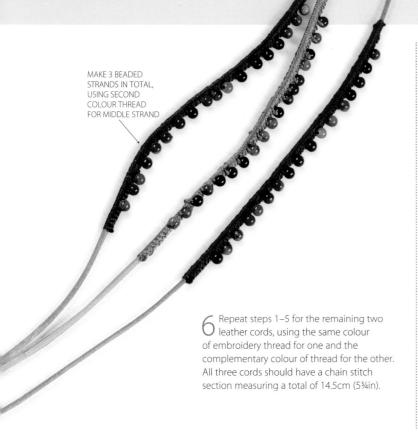

MAKE 3 BEADED
STRANDS IN TOTAL,
USING SECOND
COLOUR THREAD
FOR MIDDLE STRAND

6 Repeat steps 1–5 for the remaining two leather cords, using the same colour of embroidery thread for one and the complementary colour of thread for the other. All three cords should have a chain stitch section measuring a total of 14.5cm (5¾in).

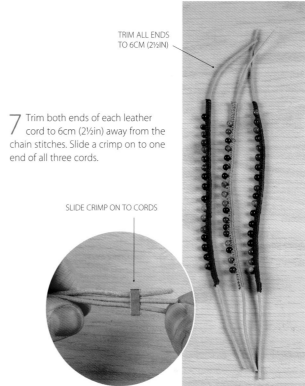

TRIM ALL ENDS
TO 6CM (2½IN)

7 Trim both ends of each leather cord to 6cm (2½in) away from the chain stitches. Slide a crimp on to one end of all three cords.

SLIDE CRIMP ON TO CORDS

BACK OF
FOCAL LINK

SLIDE CORDS THROUGH
FOCAL LINK

THREAD CORDS BACK
THROUGH CRIMP

SQUEEZE IN SIDES OF CRIMP

THEN SQUEEZE CRIMP
CLOSED FRONT TO BACK

8 Thread the cords from front to back through one end of the focal link. Take the cords back through the crimp. In order to fit the cords through, you may need to open up the crimp at the back. Make sure that the crimp overlaps the very end of the chain stitches, and then squeeze the crimp closed with chain-nose pliers to secure. For rectangular crimps, it helps to squeeze the sides in a little bit before clamping front to back. Trim away the excess leather cord. Repeat this process at the other end, taking care not to twist the leather cords.

Size
19cm (7½in) long

Materials

Two 117cm (46in) lengths of 0.5mm round leather cord

One 127cm (50in) length of 0.5mm round leather cord

Thirty gemstone chips

One 14mm two-hole button

One 6 x 4mm rectangular metal crimp

Toolkit

Ruler

Scissors

Chain-nose pliers

Tape

BEACHCOMBER CUFF

This lightweight bracelet gets its name from the mesh-like appearance created by the alternating square knots. Add gemstone chips that look like sea glass caught in the leather mesh to complete the effect.

Gemstone chips

Crimp

Button

Round leather cord

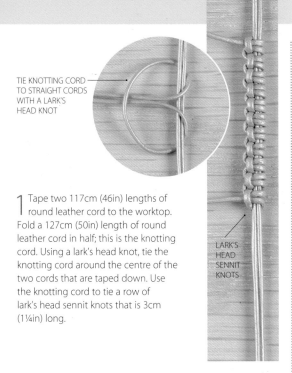

TIE KNOTTING CORD TO STRAIGHT CORDS WITH A LARK'S HEAD KNOT

LARK'S HEAD SENNIT KNOTS

1 Tape two 117cm (46in) lengths of round leather cord to the worktop. Fold a 127cm (50in) length of round leather cord in half; this is the knotting cord. Using a lark's head knot, tie the knotting cord around the centre of the two cords that are taped down. Use the knotting cord to tie a row of lark's head sennit knots that is 3cm (1¼in) long.

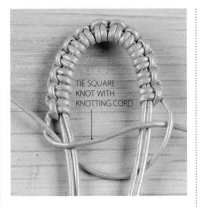

TIE SQUARE KNOT WITH KNOTTING CORD

2 Remove the project from the worktop and fold the knotted section of cord in half. Using both ends of the knotting cord, tie a square knot over the four centre cords (see page 23), just below the lark's head sennit knots, to form a button loop.

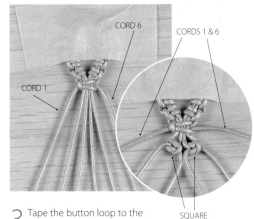

CORD 6

CORD 1

CORDS 1 & 6

SQUARE KNOTS

3 Tape the button loop to the worktop, leaving space to knot. Spread all the cords out flat. The cords are numbered 1–6 from left to right. Make a row of square knots, knotting together cords 2 & 3 and cords 4 & 5.

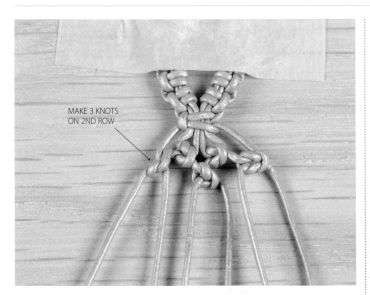

MAKE 3 KNOTS ON 2ND ROW

4 Make a row of square knots about 6mm (¼in) below the first row, knotting together cords 1 & 2, 3 & 4 and 5 & 6.

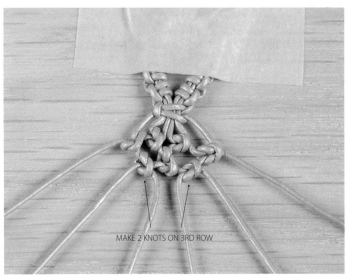

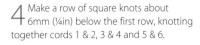

MAKE 2 KNOTS ON 3RD ROW

5 Form another row of square knots using cords 2 & 3 and 4 & 5.

STRING GEMSTONES
ON TO CORDS 1, 3 & 5

SPACE THE
STONES WITH
KNOTS

SQUARE
KNOT

6 Add a gemstone chip to cords 1, 3 and 5. Form another row of square knots, this time knotting together cords 1 & 2, 3 & 4 and 5 & 6. Space the rows of square knots about 13mm (½in) apart. Repeat steps 5–6 until the bracelet measures 18cm (7in) from the end of the button loop.

7 Use cords 1 & 6 to form a square knot over the four middle cords.

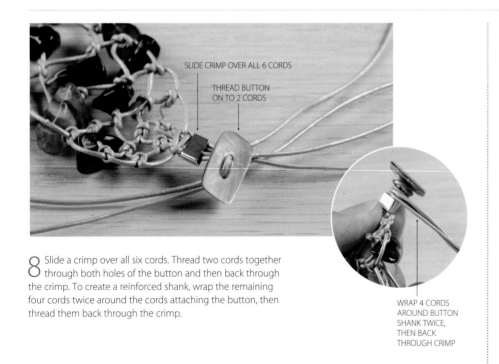

SLIDE CRIMP OVER ALL 6 CORDS

THREAD BUTTON
ON TO 2 CORDS

WRAP 4 CORDS
AROUND BUTTON
SHANK TWICE,
THEN BACK
THROUGH CRIMP

SQUEEZE CRIMP
CLOSED

8 Slide a crimp over all six cords. Thread two cords together through both holes of the button and then back through the crimp. To create a reinforced shank, wrap the remaining four cords twice around the cords attaching the button, then thread them back through the crimp.

9 Use chain-nose pliers to squeeze the crimp in place, and then trim the excess cord.

Seed beads

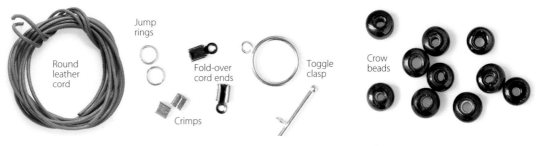

Round leather cord

Jump rings

Fold-over cord ends

Crimps

Toggle clasp

Crow beads

JOSEPHINE NECKLACE

The Josephine knot is an elaborate decorative knot that may look intimidating at first, but when broken down step by step, it will not seem difficult at all. Intricate beading at the sides of the knot give the necklace an even more elaborate look that will impress your friends.

Size

51cm (20in) long

Materials

Three 76cm (30in) lengths of 1mm round leather cord

Ninety #6 glass seed beads

Ten 9 x 6mm glass crow beads

Two 9 x 3mm fold-over cord ends

Two 4 x 4mm square metal crimps

One 16mm toggle clasp

Two 6mm jump rings

Toolkit

Ruler

Scissors

Chain-nose pliers

Tape

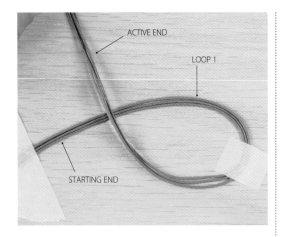

1 Line up the three lengths of round leather cord and fold them in half, creating a clockwise loop with the active end passing over the starting end. This is loop 1. Tape the starting end of the cord and the loop down on to the worktop.

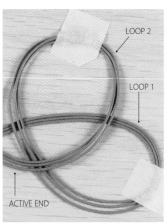

2 With the active end, form another clockwise loop perpendicular to loop 1. Loop 2 lies on top of loop 1. Pass the active end under the starting end of the cords. Tape down loop 2 to hold it in place.

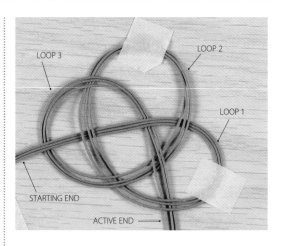

3 The final loop of the Josephine knot is woven from left to right through the previous two loops. Pass the active end over the left side of loop 2, under the left side of loop 1, over the right side of loop 2 and then under the right side of loop 1.

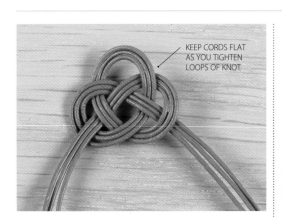

4 Remove the project from the worktop and gently pull the cords to tighten the knot, making sure that the cords remain flat and do not twist.

5 Slide a crimp on to all three cords at each side of the knot and squeeze them closed using chain-nose pliers.

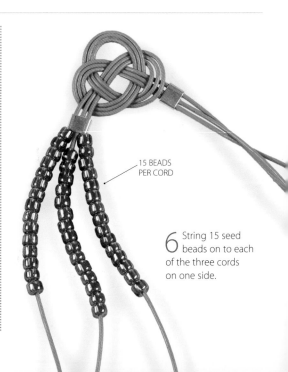

6 String 15 seed beads on to each of the three cords on one side.

BRAID THE BEADED STRANDS

20CM (8IN) PLAIN AND BEADED BRAID

8 Once the beaded section is finished, tighten the braid up to hold the beads in place and then continue until the braid measures 20cm (8in) in total, including the beaded section. Wrap a small piece of tape around the end of the braid and cut at a 45-degree angle to form a 'needle' for stringing on more beads.

TAPE END OF BRAID AND TRIM AT AN ANGLE TO FORM 'NEEDLE'

7 Hold the beads against the crimp and begin a simple three-strand braid. This braid should be looser than normal so that the beads lie nicely and are not crunched together.

CROW BEAD

FOLD-OVER CORD END

TOGGLE

RING SIDE OF CLASP

JUMP RING

JUMP RING

9 String five crow beads on to the braid and push them up to the end of the seed bead section.

10 Repeat steps 6–9 for the other side of the leather cords.

11 Trim away the point of the taped end and crimp a fold-over cord end over the end of the braid using chain-nose pliers. Repeat for the other side.

12 Use jump rings to attach a toggle clasp to the fold-over cord ends to complete.

MIXED TECHNIQUES

Mixing techniques will challenge your jewellery-making skills, and when finished, you will have an impressive and unique piece of jewellery. When you add a braid to a woven project, or mix weaving and macramé in the same piece, the result is dynamic and striking. Simple is not always better when it comes to statement jewellery. These final necklaces and bracelets mix two or three different techniques from the earlier sections, and give you a chance to put your newly learned skills to the test.

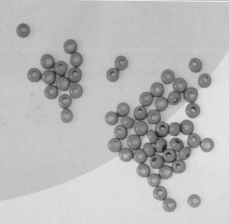

WANDERLUST NECKLACE

This necklace is sure to turn heads with its unique breastplate, or ladder styling. Beaded strands drape gracefully from braided side pieces that are also embellished with beading.

Materials

Three 1.8m (2yd) lengths of 3mm flat leather lace

Twenty-six 7 x 2mm large-hole metal rondelle beads

One hank of #3 metallic bugle beads

Two 1.8m (2yd) cards of #4 silk thread with needle

Toolkit

Ruler

Scissors

Tape

Glue

Rondelle beads

Silk thread

Bugle beads

Flat leather lace

Size
91cm (36in) long

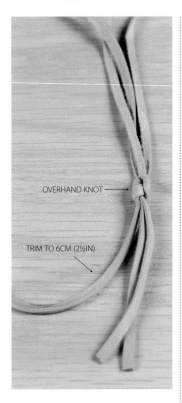

OVERHAND KNOT

TRIM TO 6CM (2½IN)

1 Line up three lengths of flat leather lace and tie an overhand knot 6cm (2½in) from one end. Trim the ends so that they are even.

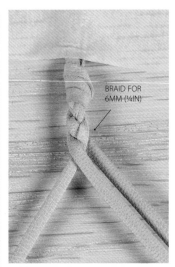

BRAID FOR 6MM (¼IN)

RONDELLE BEAD

FIRST 7.5CM (3IN) BEADED SECTION

2 Tape the trimmed end down to the worktop and begin making a simple three-strand braid on the other side of the knot. Keep the laces flat as you braid for a clean look. After the first 6mm (¼in), add a rondelle to the next left lace that comes into play. Add another rondelle every time the left strand is braided until 13 rondelles have been added and the beaded section is 7.5cm (3in) long.

64CM (25IN) PLAIN BRAID

SECOND 7.5CM (3IN) BEADED SECTION

3 Continue braiding a plain section without beads for another 64cm (25in). Then start adding rondelles again every time the left strand comes into play for another 7.5cm (3in) section to match the first rondelle section. After the last bead has been added, braid another 6mm (¼in) plain section and then tie an overhand knot to complete.

4 Trim the second side tassel 6cm (2½in) from the knot. Fold the long plain braid in half, with the fold at the top and lining up the beaded sections. Make sure the braid is not twisted. Leave an 11.5cm (4½in) space between the beaded braids at the bottom.

5 Use the needle to draw the end of the silk thread through the loops of the left-hand braid adjacent to the top of the beaded section. Tie the thread to the inside loop of the braid, taking care not to crunch the leather in the knot. Seal the knot with glue and trim off the excess thread.

TIE AND GLUE SILK THREAD TO INSIDE LOOP OF BRAID

ATTACH SILK THREAD HERE IN STEP 5

11.5CM (4½IN) SPACE BETWEEN BEADED SECTIONS

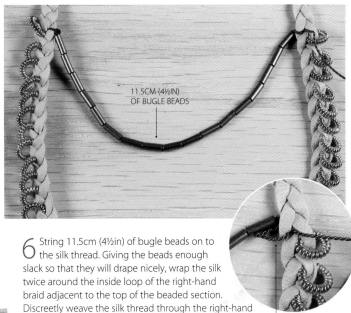

11.5CM (4½IN) OF BUGLE BEADS

KNOT, GLUE AND TRIM END OF THREAD

6 String 11.5cm (4½in) of bugle beads on to the silk thread. Giving the beads enough slack so that they will drape nicely, wrap the silk twice around the inside loop of the right-hand braid adjacent to the top of the beaded section. Discreetly weave the silk thread through the right-hand braid to the next loop down and wrap around the leather twice. String another 11.5cm (4½in) of bugle beads on to the silk and wrap the thread around the next inside loop on the left-hand braid.

JOIN STRINGS OF BEADS TO INSIDE LOOPS OF BRAIDS

7 Continue this process until you reach the end of the beaded braid sections, about 6mm (¼in) away from the knots. Tie off the silk thread, being careful not to crunch the leather. Seal the knot with glue and trim away the extra to complete.

Materials

One 3.2m (10½ft) length of 0.5mm round leather cord

One 1.4m (4½ft) length of 0.5mm round leather cord

#6 coloured glass seed beads

#6 metallic glass seed beads

One 1.8m (2yd) card of #4 or 0.6mm nylon thread with needle

One 15mm two-hole button

One 6 x 4mm rectangular metal crimp

Toolkit

Ruler

Scissors

Chain-nose pliers

Thread burner

Tape

SUMMER WIND WRAP BRACELET

Wrap bracelets are a great place to play with mixing and matching techniques, because you can get the look of wearing multiple bracelets with just one. This double-wrap bracelet alternates sections of beaded square knots and bead weaving, and is finished off with a button and bound button-loop closure.

Crimp

Coloured seed beads

Nylon thread

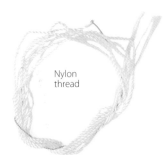

Button

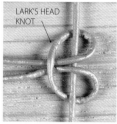

LARK'S HEAD KNOT

LARK'S HEAD SENNIT KNOT

3CM (1¼IN) ROW OF KNOTS

1 Tape a 1.4m (4½ft) length of round leather cord to the worktop. Fold a 3.2m (10½ft) length of round leather cord and form a lark's head knot (see page 21) over the centre of the cord that is taped down. Form a row of lark's head sennit knots (see page 22) that measures 3cm (1¼in) long using the knotting cord.

BUTTON LOOP

SQUARE KNOT

2 Remove the project from the worktop and fold the knotted section of cord in half. Using both ends of the knotting cord, make a square knot (see page 23) over the two centre cords to form a button loop.

3 Tape the button loop and the two centre cords to the worktop, leaving space to knot. Add a metallic seed bead to each of the knotting cords. Slide the beads up to the last knot and form another square knot. Repeat this process for about 2.5cm (1in). The beads will sit on the outside of the knots.

Metallic seed beads

Round leather cord

1 METALLIC SEED BEAD ON EACH KNOTTING CORD

TIE A SQUARE KNOT

PULL KNOT TIGHT UP TO BEADS

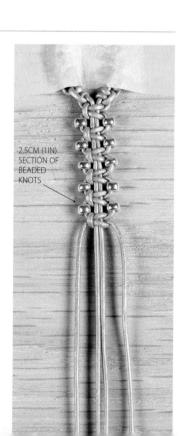

2.5CM (1IN) SECTION OF BEADED KNOTS

SECURE NYLON
THREAD TO
LEFT CORD

4 Separate out all the cords and tape them down to the
worktop. Tie the end of the nylon thread to the left-hand
cord and seal the knot with a thread burner.

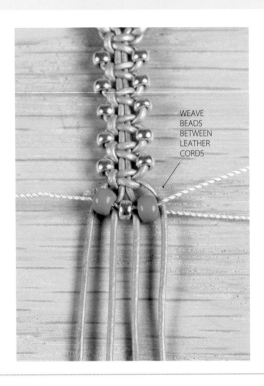

WEAVE
BEADS
BETWEEN
LEATHER
CORDS

5 Add 1 coloured, 1 metallic and
1 coloured seed bead to the nylon
thread. Pass the nylon thread under all
four leather cords from left to right,
placing one bead between each pair
of cords. Thread the needle back
through all three beads, coming over
the leather cords from right to left this
time, and pull the thread snug.

SEAL END
OF THREAD

6 Repeat step 5 until the woven
section measures 9cm (3½in).
Tie off the nylon thread and seal
the knot with a thread burner.

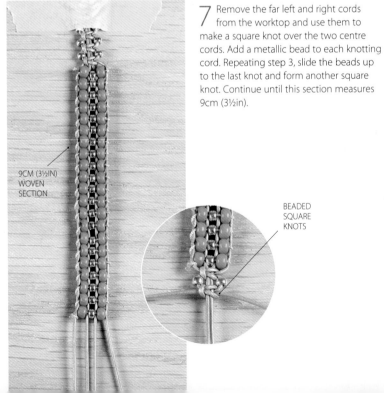

9CM (3½IN)
WOVEN
SECTION

BEADED
SQUARE
KNOTS

7 Remove the far left and right cords
from the worktop and use them to
make a square knot over the two centre
cords. Add a metallic bead to each knotting
cord. Repeating step 3, slide the beads up
to the last knot and form another square
knot. Continue until this section measures
9cm (3½in).

9CM (3½IN)
SECTION
OF BEADED
KNOTS

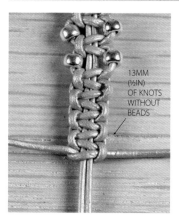

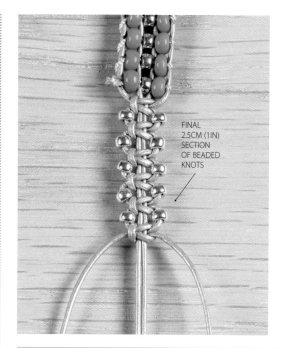

9CM
(3½IN)
SECTION
OF BEADED
KNOTS

8 Spread out all four cords and tape them to the worktop once again. Tie the end of the nylon thread to the far left cord and seal the knot with a thread burner. Repeat step 5 to form another 9cm (3½in) woven section. Tie off the nylon cord and seal with the thread burner.

FINAL
2.5CM (1IN)
SECTION
OF BEADED
KNOTS

9 Remove the far left and right cords from the worktop again and form a square knot over the two centre cords. Add a metallic seed bead to each of the knotting cords and repeat step 3 until you have a section that measures 2.5cm (1in).

SECOND
9CM
(3½IN)
WOVEN
SECTION

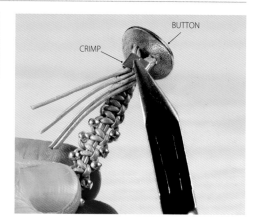

13MM
(½IN)
OF KNOTS
WITHOUT
BEADS

10 Continue to form square knots without beads for 13mm (½in). This will create a shank for the button.

BUTTON

CRIMP

11 Remove the project from the worktop and slide a crimp on to all four cords right against the last square knot. Thread the ends of the cords through the holes of the button and back through the crimp. Use chain-nose pliers to squeeze the crimp down on to the cords, then trim away the excess cord close to the crimp.

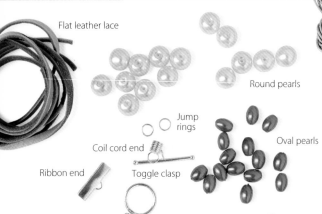

Flat leather lace

Round pearls

Round leather cord

Jump rings

Oval pearls

Coil cord end

Ribbon end

Toggle clasp

Materials

Five 168cm (66in) lengths of 0.5mm round leather cord

Two 152cm (60in) lengths of 3mm flat deer-hide leather lace

One 40cm (16in) strand of 10mm round glass pearl beads

Two 40cm (16in) strands of 8 x 6mm oval glass pearl beads

One coil cord end

One 19 x 5mm ribbon end

One 16mm toggle clasp

Two 6mm jump rings

Toolkit

Ruler

Scissors

Chain-nose pliers

Tape

Size
74cm (29in) outside; 60cm (24in) inside

DAYDREAMER NECKLACE

A statement necklace can seem like an intimidating project to take on, but when it is broken down into its individual parts, it becomes much more manageable. This long five-strand necklace is done in a bib style, with a large braid at the back and individual draped strands at the front that are either braided or knotted with beads.

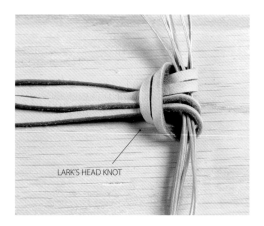

LARK'S HEAD KNOT

FISHTAIL BRAID

1 Line up the five lengths of round leather cord. Next, line up the two lengths of flat leather lace, then fold them in half and form a lark's head knot over the centre of the round cords (see page 21).

2 Using the flat leather lace, make a four-strand fishtail braid (see page 25). Make sure that the strands remain flat when braiding for a clean look.

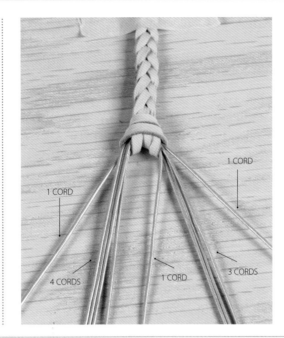

4 Tape the starting end of the braided leather lace section to the worktop. Separate out the 10 round leather cords into the following groups from left to right: 1 cord, 4 cords, 1 cord, 3 cords, 1 cord.

1 CORD

1 CORD

4 CORDS

1 CORD

3 CORDS

3 Continue until the braid is 36cm (14in) long. When finished, tape off the end of the braid.

36CM (14IN) FISHTAIL BRAID

4 CORDS

32CM (12½IN) FISHTAIL BRAID

5 Using the group of four cords, braid a four-strand fishtail braid that measures 32cm (12½in). You may want to tape down the other cords to keep them out of the way while you work. When finished, tape off the end.

3 CORDS

6 Take the group of three cords and make a simple three-strand braid that is 24cm (9½in) long. When finished, tape off the end.

FISHTAIL BRAID

3-STRAND BRAID

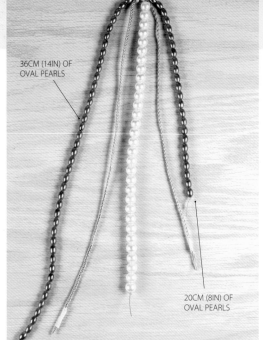

36CM (14IN) OF OVAL PEARLS

20CM (8IN) OF OVAL PEARLS

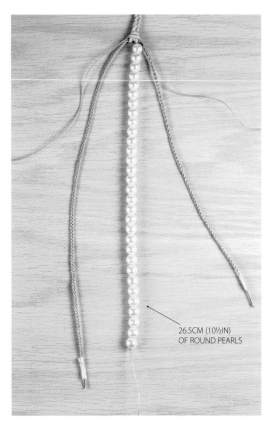

26.5CM (10½IN) OF ROUND PEARLS

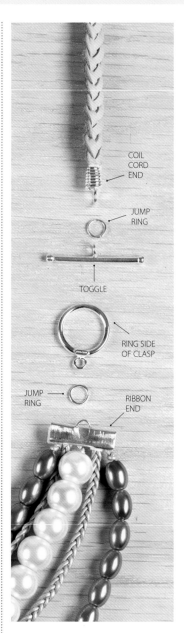

COIL CORD END

JUMP RING

TOGGLE

RING SIDE OF CLASP

JUMP RING

RIBBON END

7 On the middle cord, string 26.5cm (10½in) of round pearls and knot the end of the cord to hold the beads. String 36cm (14in) of oval pearls on to the far left single cord and knot the end. On the far right single cord, string 20cm (8in) of oval pearls and knot the end.

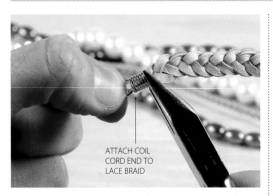

ATTACH COIL CORD END TO LACE BRAID

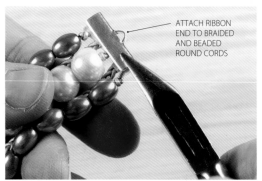

ATTACH RIBBON END TO BRAIDED AND BEADED ROUND CORDS

8 Trim the taped end of the leather lace braid and fit a coil cord end over it. Use chain-nose pliers to squeeze the last coil tight over the leather lace braid.

9 Trim the taped ends of both round cord braids and trim the beaded strands 1cm (³/₈in) away from the last knot. Line up all the ends and crimp a ribbon end over all of them using chain-nose pliers. Make sure the cords are lined up in order and do not twist around each other.

10 Use jump rings to attach the toggle side of the clasp to the braided lace end of the necklace and the ring side of the clasp to the beaded end.

Size
20cm (8in) long

TAPESTRY CUFF

A wide cuff bracelet is a great statement piece to add to your jewellery collection. This cuff layers rows of bead weaving and braiding, and is finished with a leather-bound edge and hook-and-eye clasp.

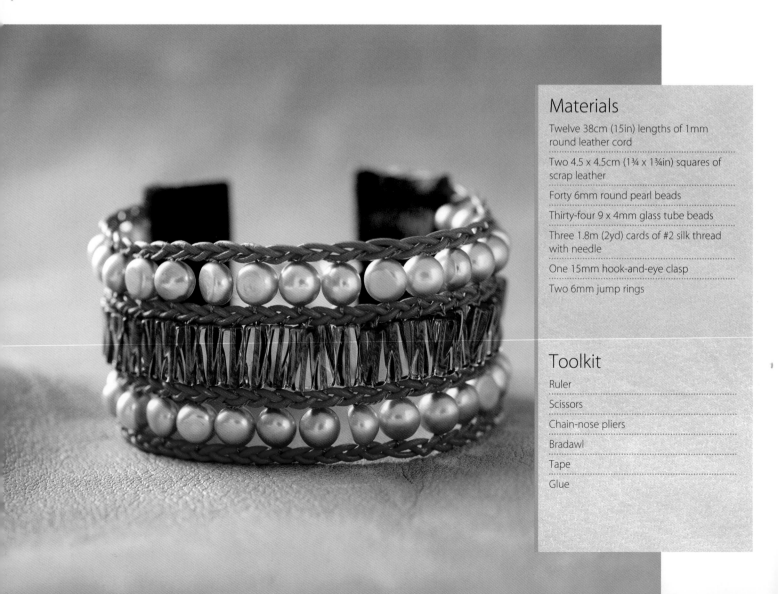

Materials

Twelve 38cm (15in) lengths of 1mm round leather cord

Two 4.5 x 4.5cm (1¾ x 1¾in) squares of scrap leather

Forty 6mm round pearl beads

Thirty-four 9 x 4mm glass tube beads

Three 1.8m (2yd) cards of #2 silk thread with needle

One 15mm hook-and-eye clasp

Two 6mm jump rings

Toolkit

Ruler

Scissors

Chain-nose pliers

Bradawl

Tape

Glue

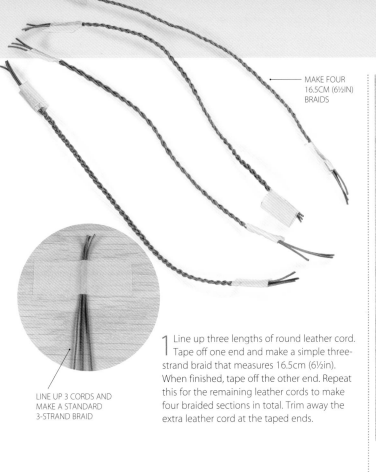

MAKE FOUR
16.5CM (6½IN)
BRAIDS

LINE UP 3 CORDS AND
MAKE A STANDARD
3-STRAND BRAID

1 Line up three lengths of round leather cord. Tape off one end and make a simple three-strand braid that measures 16.5cm (6½in). When finished, tape off the other end. Repeat this for the remaining leather cords to make four braided sections in total. Trim away the extra leather cord at the taped ends.

TAPE DOWN
AT EACH END

6MM (¼IN)
SPACE BETWEEN
PAIR OF BRAIDS

2 Lay out two of the braided sections with 6mm (¼in) between them. Tape them down to the worktop at top and bottom.

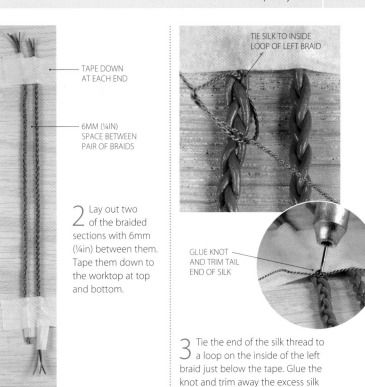

TIE SILK TO INSIDE
LOOP OF LEFT BRAID

GLUE KNOT
AND TRIM TAIL
END OF SILK

3 Tie the end of the silk thread to a loop on the inside of the left braid just below the tape. Glue the knot and trim away the excess silk at the tail end.

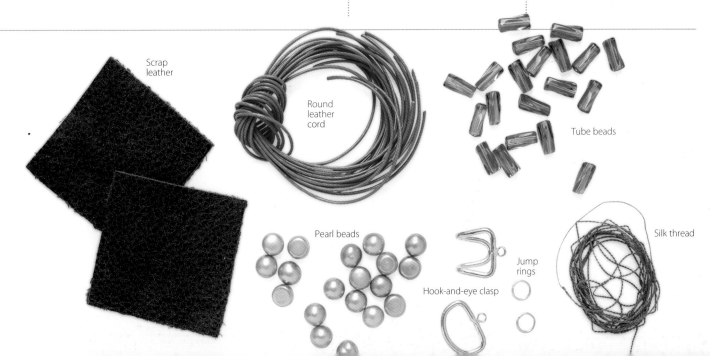

Scrap leather

Round leather cord

Tube beads

Pearl beads

Hook-and-eye clasp

Jump rings

Silk thread

4 String a pearl bead on to the silk. Slide the bead up to the left braid and then thread the silk through an inside loop on the right braid. Thread the silk back through the bead from right to left, and then thread it through the next inside loop of the left braid. Pull the silk tight. Repeat this process, lining up each pearl bead next to the one before it, until there is a woven section that measures 13cm (5¼in). Tie off the silk thread, glue the knot and trim away the excess.

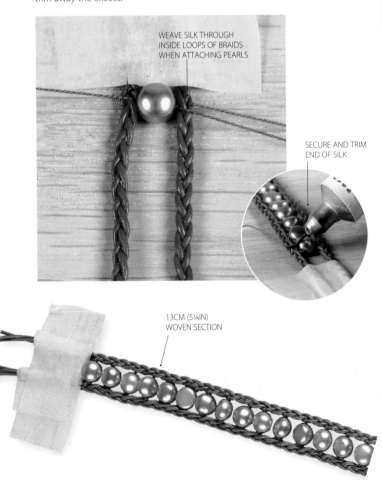

WEAVE SILK THROUGH INSIDE LOOPS OF BRAIDS WHEN ATTACHING PEARLS

SECURE AND TRIM END OF SILK

13CM (5¼IN) WOVEN SECTION

5 Repeat steps 2–4 with another two braided sections. The braided sections must be the exact same length. When finished, tape them down side by side with 1cm (³⁄₈in) between them. Tie the end of a silk thread to an inside loop on the left braided section, in line with the first pearl bead. Glue the knot and trim away excess thread.

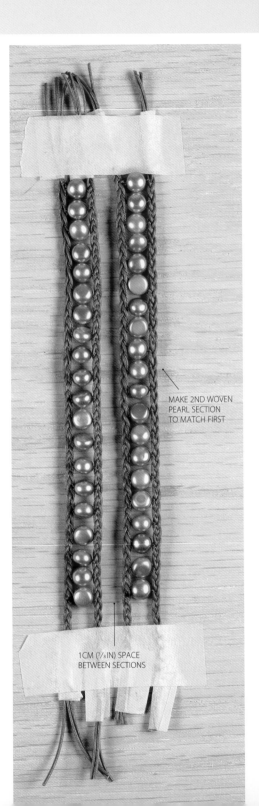

MAKE 2ND WOVEN PEARL SECTION TO MATCH FIRST

1CM (³⁄₈IN) SPACE BETWEEN SECTIONS

WEAVE TUBE BEADS BETWEEN PEARL SECTIONS

ALIGN BEADS AT EDGE OF LEATHER SQUARE

FOLD OVER LEATHER AND PRESS FIRMLY

6 String a tube bead on to the silk thread. Slide the bead up to the left braided section and then thread the silk through an inside loop on the right braided section. Thread the silk back through the tube bead from right to left, and then thread it through an inside loop of the left braided section. Pull the silk tight. Repeat this process, weaving each tube next to the one before it, until the centre woven section is the same length as the pearl sections at the sides. Tie off the silk, glue the knot and trim away the excess.

7 Run glue all along the inside of one square of scrap leather. Place one end of the woven bracelet on top so that the last beads are at the edge of the leather. Fold over the leather, lining it up edge to edge, and press firmly until the glue sets. Repeat at the other end.

SECURE END OF SILK AS BEFORE

USE A BRADAWL TO MAKE A HOLE NEAR THE CENTRE EDGE

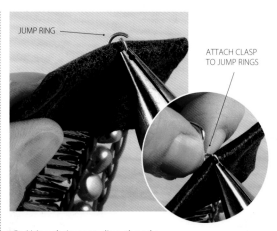

JUMP RING

ATTACH CLASP TO JUMP RINGS

8 Find the centre of the leather binding and use a bradawl to poke a hole through both layers about 3mm (1/8in) from the edge. Repeat at the other end.

9 Using chain-nose pliers, thread a jump ring through each hole and attach the clasp.

Materials

Three 86cm (34in) lengths of 3mm flat leather lace

Nine 30cm (12in) strands of 0.5mm round leather cord

#6 glass seed beads

Two coil cord ends

One 10 x 6mm lobster clasp

One 6mm jump ring

Toolkit

Ruler

Scissors

Chain-nose pliers

Bradawl

Tape

Size

40cm (16in) long with 6cm (2½in) fringe

AMAZON COLLAR

For an intricate look, try mixing three techniques to make this fringed choker. The base of the necklace is a simple braid, but at the front is a macramé lace-like pattern with a beaded fringe hanging from it.

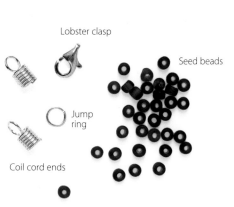

Lobster clasp

Jump ring

Coil cord ends

Seed beads

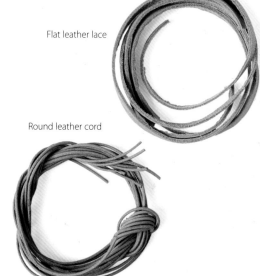

Flat leather lace

Round leather cord

40CM (16IN)
LEATHER LACE
BRAID

1 Line up the three lengths of flat leather lace and tape down one end. Make a simple three-strand braid measuring 40cm (16in). Keep the laces flat as you braid for a clean look. When finished, tape off the other end.

USE A BRADAWL TO TEASE OPEN CENTRE OF BRAID

SLIP FOLDED CORD THROUGH BRAID

LARK'S HEAD KNOT

2 Find the centre of the braid and use a bradawl to gently tease open the loop at the centre just enough to fit a thin cord through. Fold one strand of the round leather cord in half and slip the folded end, from front to back, through the teased-open loop in the braid. Remove the bradawl and pull the tail ends of the cord through the folded end to form a lark's head knot (see page 21).

TIE ANOTHER CORD TO LEFT OF CENTRE

TIE ANOTHER CORD TO RIGHT OF CENTRE

3 Use the bradawl to tease open a loop to the right of the first and repeat step 2, using another piece of round cord to form a lark's head knot through the braid. Repeat this process on the next loop to the left of the centre, and form another lark's head knot using another round cord.

THERE WILL BE 18 CORD ENDS WHEN YOU FINISH

4 Alternating to the left and right of centre, repeat this process for all nine round cords.

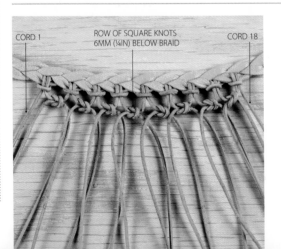

CORD 1

ROW OF SQUARE KNOTS 6MM (¼IN) BELOW BRAID

CORD 18

5 When finished, lay out all 18 ends of cord. From left to right, the cords are numbered 1–18. Begin by making a row of square knots by knotting together cords 2 & 3, 4 & 5, 6 & 7, 8 & 9, 10 & 11, 12 & 13, 14 & 15 and finally 16 & 17 (see page 23). These knots should be about 6mm (¼in) away from the braid.

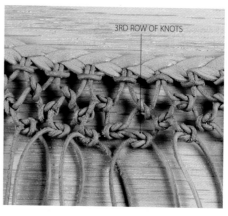

6 Make a second row of square knots, this time shifting the pairs of cords over by one cord to the left – that is, knot cords 1 & 2, 3 & 4, 5 & 6, 7 & 8, 9 & 10, 11 & 12, 13 & 14, 15 & 16 and finally 17 & 18. These knots should be about 6mm (¼in) away from the first row.

2ND ROW OF KNOTS START THE LACE-LIKE TRELLIS PATTERN

3RD ROW OF KNOTS

7 Make a third row of square knots following the pattern in step 5. This row should be about 6mm (¼in) away from the second row.

5CM (2IN) OF BEADS PER CORD

KNOT AND TRIM ENDS

COIL CORD END

9 Remove the necklace from the worktop and trim the taped ends of the braid to 1cm (³⁄₈in). Crimp a coil cord end over each side of the flat braid using chain-nose pliers.

LOBSTER CLASP

JUMP RING

10 Attach a lobster clasp to the right end of the leather braid and a jump ring to the left end to finish the necklace.

8 String 5cm (2in) of seed beads on to each of the cords and tie each cord with an overhand knot. Trim the extra cord to 6mm (¼in).

INDEX

CREDITS

SUPPLIERS
www.beadworks.com
www.firemountaingems.com
www.leathercordusa.com
www.riogrande.com

AUTHOR'S ACKNOWLEDGEMENTS
I want to thank my friends and family for being so supportive of me and pushing me to follow my dreams wherever they lead. I want to thank my husband, Devin Sidell, for being my cheerleader through everything. I would not have had the courage to take on this project and start my business without him. To my parents, Rick and Ceil Horn, for encouraging me to take on the challenge of writing this book and showing me what it takes to be an entrepreneur. To all of my mentors over the years, including Joanne Standfast, Beth Young, Kim Montenegro, Susan Rifkin and many others, who have taught me the skills I've needed to get where I am today. Thank you to the team at Quarto, who found my little shop on Etsy and were so wonderful to work with on this book. I could not have done this without all of you. And I want especially to thank everyone who supports the handmade movement all over the world – you help to keep the art of craft alive and well in our modern age.